A FAR CRY FROM PLYMOUTH ROCK

ALSO BY KWAME DAWES

KWAME DAWES

A FAR CRY FROM PLYMOUTH ROCK

a personal narrative

PEEPAL TREE

First published in Great Britain in 2007
Peepal Tree Press Ltd
17 King's Avenue
Leeds LS6 1QS
UK

ISBN 1 84523 025 6
ISBN13: 9 781 84523 025 8

Peepal Tree gratefully acknowledges Arts Council support

CONTENTS

for Lorna

Sena, Kekeli and Akua

and for

Mama, the Great

Gwyneth, Kojo, Aba, Adjoa, Kojovi

remembering Neville

CHAPTER 1

'o dreams, o destinations'

I never planned to make America the subject of an entire book; this would be offering undue attention to a country that did not need me to speak of it. I never expected America to be important to me in intimate and complex ways. I had approached America in simple, rhetorical terms – the terms of anti-imperialist dogma. But then, I never expected to live in America. Now I do, and being in America has forced me to re-evaluate, to reconfigure my sense of who I am.

I am involved in America. I teach in an American institution, I go to an American church, I have American children and I watch American television. I now know the names of American plants and bushes. America has entered my psyche, my imagination. I write poems about America, I get involved in American habits like pretending there is an immense difference between Democrats and Republicans. I no longer do things like follow the march of test cricket because, somehow, cricket has faded as a definer of who I am.

It is true that I cling, like many reluctant immigrants, to the fantasy that someday soon I will leave this Babylon and return home to the Promised Land to live out the balance of my days. I know this is a fantasy. The pragmatics of American living make it possible to imagine that one day I might try to be naturalized; I might choose to secure an American passport and, once and for all, spit on my father's grave. This is, of course, melodramatic. My father has no grave; he was cremated and his ashes are still, as far as I know, in an urn in a vault or on a shelf in a funeral home in downtown Kingston. It is all melodrama. Spitting on graves is not something I make a habit of. It just sounds dramatic and funny. But my becoming an American *might* have bothered my father were he alive. He would probably have understood the pragmatics of the action, but he would have seen it, I am sure, as a failure on his part. Or perhaps he would have blamed me for failing him, for not living up to his expectations. He would never have said it – that was never his way – but he would have felt it. The fact is that living in America represents a break from my father and his spirit.

But then my father was not always a practical person. My mother called him a dreamer. She meant an idealist, but his idealism was of a complicated sort. He did not fit the typical image of a dreamer: an underachieving, deficient person whose prospects of success are, more often than not, hopeless. My father was a successful man. He did things. He was known. Sometimes he actually got away with the self-assured and arrogant declaration: "Do you know who I am?" I have witnessed people scrambling at the recognition of his name. We – my brothers and sisters – must all have witnessed such an occasion; it is the only way to explain why each of us has his or her account of how we used those same words. We all remain embarrassed by our less than successful attempts at self-assertion, but my father could do this and get away with it.

My father's significance in my life must already be evident, but he had no fanciful notions about fatherhood. True, we called him "Neville" – and apparently, for a few years in our childhood, we referred to our mother as "Chochoo". An aunt quickly and earnestly disabused us of that tendency. I can remember learning to say "Mama" and finding the process strange, even though

I can't actually remember calling my mother "Chochoo". If our aunt, an enthusiastic close friend of the family, whom we called, reverentially, Aunty Rosa, had attempted to get us to discard "Neville" and replace it with Daddy" or "Papa", she failed. She must have failed, because in my memory the word "Daddy" has no meaning, no resonance. Whatever significance it has for me today is explained by the fact that my children call me "Daddy". But as a child and during my teenage years, the term "Daddy" seemed silly, affected, bourgeois, pretentious, and American. I realized, though, by the time I was eleven, that my friends found my calling my father Neville extremely odd. For them, my father was a bit of an eccentric for allowing this. True, he was stern and only muttered monosyllabic replies when I would ask him if we could give some friends a lift when I was picked up at school in the Institute of Jamaica's VW van, driven by the geriatric but endearing Mr. Jones. My father was aloof. He perfected aloofness. I know it to have been shyness. It is a trait I have inherited. I am called aloof, especially at times when I am squirming with anxiety about what to say.

Perhaps letting us call him "Neville" was part of his idealism, his liberal manner, but we never felt calling him that was a privilege. It was all we knew. "Neville" was equivalent to "Daddy" – it had the same qualities. We said "Neville", not with the sense of familiarity, of using his first name, but with a burden of respect, awe, and submission. We were disciplined children; we were not pals with our parents. These days, that might suggest something distant or cold; but it was neither of those things. It was about knowing boundaries and understanding the difference between adults and children.

When Oprah Winfrey declares that children are not kids but "little people" or "little adults", it is obvious that she has no children or that she is overcompensating for the abuses that some children face. But we *were* children and we understood the difference and somehow appreciated it. Adults drank coffee;

9

children did not. I, quite clearly, never grew up, for coffee has gone the way of cigarettes and alcohol: stuff adults do. My father was not a fanciful dreamer when it came to his role as a father.

But he was a dreamer. His dreams became a part of the mythic lore of our family. As long as I knew him, he always had a dream about a future time, a future place for himself, for his family – for each of us. Perhaps it was the novelist and poet in him, or the part of him that was optimistic about the future, but he told us his dreams not as dreams – never as dreams – but as plans, as detailed plans for his life. He would lay out clear options and speak with assurance about making them happen. They rarely did. They were often far-fetched and yet we believed them because he believed them. Oddly, his dreams were the one place in which the stark realities of his Marxism did not play a major role. Indeed, his dreams seemed to work against some of his more obvious ideological positions. Recently, I discovered that he was always dreaming, always filled with longing for something, long before he had met my mother, long before he left Jamaica for Ghana. As I read in his letters about his old dreams, I began to understand him more.

In the early summer of 1997, I spent two days in Birmingham with a wonderful university lecturer there called Stewart Brown. The time is a blur because I did not sleep much – I spent the night writing a suite of poems based on the sculptures of Edna Manley. While the night's profusion of verse may seem to suggest that I was impassioned by some lively muse, what is truer is that Stewart had a book on Manley's art and I would not have access to it after leaving Birmingham the next day. So I wrote all night in the teddy-bear and Spice Girls paraphernalia-festooned bedroom of Stewart's daughter, who had kindly vacated it. In the morning, Stewart drove me to the train station in a slight drizzle, which made everything green even greener. As he drove, he shifted from topic to topic. I remember bits and pieces –

10

the chocolate industry and the exploitation of Africa; the poetry of Linton Kwesi Johnson; the predictions of Derek Walcott; and about meeting Evan Jones: "You must give him a ring before you go barging in on him." From Evan Jones had come the enticing tale of some letters my father had written when he was in his early- to mid-twenties at Oxford. There was some confusion about whether I would ever see the letters; I was too tired to make out the details, but I felt as if there was something good in the offing.

I got the letters three months later. I read them quickly, as if they had been written to me. I was seeing another layer of my father. I was moved, startled by what I read. My father's brand of dreaming was a cultivated art – he had been at it for years. His was an anti-colonial dream. It was a dream he would pass on to us. Its anti-imperialism inevitably touched on America. It would, therefore, come to shape my sense of America.

When I decided to accept a teaching position at the University of South Carolina, I was discarding my father's dream. This is what was at stake and this is what might have caused his soul to stay wherever it was.

What was this dream?

It varied, always varied.

It had to do with landscape, landscape in the romantic sense. In the autumn of 1997, I was in London to promote two new books and to try and make a few pounds to help keep the overdraft hounds at bay at my bank in South Carolina. The week before I left was a miserable time. My office on the second floor of the drab Humanities monolith was a mess. I had already written four lists of "to do's" and the sheets were still so tidy: a sure sign that I was not getting through anything. It was typical of my pre-departure ritual. I grow quite depressed before a long trip away from the family. It darkens everything I do. It does not matter how exciting the plans for my trip might be – I do not like being away. But this depression was compounded by the realization of how broke we were; the sheer weight of our debts and the vicious tyranny of service charges for each overdrawn cheque was burying us in an impossible hole. I was travelling for money. It was as simple as that. I talked to my agents in the States – a term of faith because at the time we had sold nothing. I needed to pass on to them my desperation to be a success – a financial success with a book sold. They were gentle. I promised to get material to them. They were gentle. I grew more depressed when I hung up after each conversation.

On the Wednesday night before my departure, I was to do a reading at a small cafe in Columbia called the 'Alley Cat'. It was an old commitment I had made to one of my students who was convinced that her poetry was far too taboo-breaking to be easily accepted at a conventional reading. She called the reading "Taboo", a forum for poets to read about taboo issues. She was never *that* shocking a poet, but it is a Northerner tendency to assume a certain liberal *savoir faire* when ensconced in the Southern Bible Belt. They like to smile conspiratorially with those done-upon by Southern ways. I tried to get out of the reading and she cried. I wanted out because I was feeling completely down about leaving, because I did not have the time and because I knew that for me "taboo" would mean poems about sex and sexuality. Such playful indulgence seemed the last thing I wanted to hinder my desperate days before departure. But I read. The truth is that the reading was a rather tame affair. I felt even worse afterwards.

London seemed uncomplicated. I arrived tired, but prepared for the toil. It was colder than in Columbia, but quite bearable. The faces on the Underground were as mute as ever. London seemed frigid; the women and men flowed past me like lumps of clothes, eyes void of intrigue and bodies strangely unaware of the language of sensuality. It was the London I knew, all over again.

Yet it may have been here that I started to rethink my father's dreamings. In 1955, after leaving Oxford to return to Jamaica to teach, he wrote to a friend in London, waxing nostalgic for that world. I could tell that he loved England, loved the scent, the cool, the cricket, and the cultured world of Oxford. Two things happened while I was in London that drew me back to my father's dream and how I would come to inherit it and then reject it.

The night of my arrival in London involved a reading at the Lewisham Theatre. This grand event was an indiscriminate parade of Black British male "voices", each spending five minutes on stage, "performing". The event was absurd for, on one level, it had some of the leading Black British writers, and yet no one would have known this judging from the ignorance of the MCs about who was performing. I would spend days harping on about the sheer disrespect shown to writers like Linton Kwesi Johnson and Mike Phillips, while other performers forcefully demanded an undeserved adulation for the kind of self-indulgent clichés produced by "freedom struggles" anywhere. Backstage was more interesting.

Backstage was Jean Binta Breeze, stopping by during a European tour. With her was Ibo Cooper of Third World. With a slight paunch and a strangely domestic roundness and softness of body, he seemed more jolly than dangerously reggae. But there was also a man called Ian Hall who came to introduce himself. Coming out of an Afro-Guyanese man, his accent was startling. It was a thoroughly Oxford accent. I was startled because it sounded so familiar. It was the sound and manner of my father. Neville Dawes's Oxford breeding made me wonder what exactly happened at that school. Did they have elocution lessons? Did they punish them for not speaking in this way? Was this voluntary "breeding"? My father's Oxford friends had similar accents, but those younger than he was did not. Mervyn Morris has no trace of Oxford in his accent, and Rex Nettleford has to make an effort, but E.V. Ellington's Oxford tones were thickly laid on and so was the accent of other men in my father's generation.

Ian Hall's accent was uncompromising, so much so that it caused some of the men in the dressing room to stare. It seemed incongruous, but it was what I grew up with. In retrospect, it is curious how my father, a committed Pan-Africanist with a strong sense of blackness, and no patience with the racist delusions of whites, would adopt so thoroughly the dialect of empire. It still seems quite misguided. That is until it is connected with his dreams, his nostalgia for Oxford and the way he negotiated these issues in his life. My father could have been called an Anglophile. He sounded like one, but his passion against imperialism and his devotion to an anti-colonial agenda was total. But he loved England. He did. And he, like a truly English person, was suspicious of America. It is impossible to understand how these contradictory impulses came about, and I can only safely talk about how they affected my own perceptions of these various places.

My youthful romanticism about England came from my father. It was his dream. With real contact, this romantic sense of England would fade. It had happened even before the 1997 visit. But it took America to push it wholly from my imagination. It took living, working, and raising a family in America for me to see this romantic notion had gone. This was disturbing and painful because I feared that I was replacing it with something American. I am not sure how exactly it happened, but there was a definite fissure, a divide that emerged. I would date this to 1994 when I realised that the England I was visiting was quite different from the England I had in my head: an England of the early '70s, and 1986-90. I was not in England between 1986 and 1990, but my wife-to-be was, and our long-distance romance was marked by our long letters, long telephone calls, and her occasional visits to Canada, where I was studying. So, before I came in 1994, London was still loaded with tangible memories of my childhood and the complex emotions of my early adulthood.

For years, England had been a place of possibility. That was my father's dream. We would be at university in England, while he would buy a nice cottage in Oxford, where he would teach a little and spend his days writing the great Ghana-based novel he claimed to be writing. You could tell how totally it was a dream because even my eldest brother, Kojo, featured prominently. Kojo had not got particularly good 'O' level results, so after Jamaica College he had gone to work at the Institute of Jamaica. Despite his industry, there was always the feeling that he needed to get a university degree. For years, his dream was to do Law. My father absorbed this dream into his grand plan. It would all take place in England. We joined the dream: the trips to Europe, the wonderful English sweets, fish and chips and the like. We had a vivid picture of that life of ours.

My mother listened indulgently and would never pooh-pooh anything he said. I am sure she knew he was dreaming, but my father's dreams were so seductive that sometimes, I am certain, she was drawn into them.

We, his children, believed in the myths thoroughly. I certainly did. In Ghana, the dream was not about England. It was about Jamaica. My father always talked about Jamaica, about our going to Jamaica. This meant that for the first eight years of my life, which were spent in Ghana, I always had the sense of being only temporarily there, of being about to leave. Now, as I look back, I realize there has always been this sense of being unsettled, of being an alien, only "kotching" in one place for a while before moving on to another place, then another.

So in Ghana, the promised land was Jamaica. My father would tell us stories about growing up in Jamaica. For us, Jamaica was a grand country town where children got to ride donkeys, barbecue pimento, sprint through hilly terrain, attend boarding schools where cricket was played and where teachers were "masters", eat mangoes growing abundantly on the trees all about the village and, on a clear day, see Cuba across the sea. He told us jokes and stories from Jamaica. He recited over and over again Jamaican poems, like his good friend Evan Jones's "Song of the Banana Man":

> Yes by God and his big right hand
> I will live and die a banana man.

Anancy the trickster spider figured in these stories, as did ghosts and rolling calves, rum, molasses and sugar. Jamaica was green, we thought; Jamaica would be our point of arrival and our proper setting. He was a good word-weaver and managed over the years to plant a strange seed of restlessness in us that made it a foregone conclusion that one day we would leave Ghana, leave our friends, our cousins, our familiar paths, and enter a completely new world.

From those early days, then, I lived with the mind of an immigrant. The prospect of travel was my future. And travel, indeed, was a normal part of our lives. I was four when the family travelled to the Caribbean for the first time. We were briefly in Jamaica, but then spent most of that year in Guyana, where my father was guest chair at the English Department of the newly established University of Guyana. It would be an important trip because it included my first time in America.

At this time, my father's eldest sister, Flo, lived in New York. Unlike her younger brother, her success had not taken her to England. She did not have his quintessential colonial dream: to study in the motherland, to shine at the best university in the English-speaking world and play cricket there. I have the feeling that my father was the favoured and pampered one in his family. He was the youngest. He had a brother and two sisters. The brother, Winston, became a barrister and remained

16

in Jamaica, apparently squandering the family's fortune which, we were assured by my mother, who found out these things, had included five expensive houses in Kingston, much land in St. Anns, and other untold holdings. Like much about my father's side of the family, this propertied and settled gentrified status was something we never quite inherited. Winston was an alcoholic and he died not long after a few years of living with us, after we had moved to Jamaica.

My grandfather was a disciplined teacher and an elegant preacher who wrote a daily journal detailing the routine of his days with military precision. The care for each penny earned and spent was evident in the careful accounting that formed part of his entries. These also included small verses, some he wrote and others he remembered. He played village cricket, gave sermons of beauty and power and managed to do a sensible job of building the family's circumstances after they returned to Jamaica after fifteen years in the mission field in Nigeria. My father came from a family aware of its Africanness and yet quite clearly shaped by the strictures and codes of colonial Victorian society. I have always imagined him going to the country cricket grounds in St. Ann with his father to play lively games of cricket. In one entry in 1937, my grandfather records that 'Nev' made 11 runs and took two wickets. The details of the rest of the match were omitted. My father may have been favoured as the last child, but he was the son of a man of serious thought and discipline. If siblings did well by the old man, they got property or were supported in their academic ventures, and all had tertiary education and professional lives. My father, though, was the one who got to Oxford, who was a great cricketer and who, it seems, felt he deserved the support he received. I never met my grandfather. He died at least fifteen years before I was born, but he returns to me as a fascinating ancestor.

The details of my father's relationship with his siblings were not accessible. They were a black middle-class and aspiring

17

Jamaican family, closed-up and reticent. I can only grasp at tiny speculations and the threads of overheard conversations and a few piles of airmail letters mailed between Jamaica and England in the fifties. From these it was clear that Neville's going to Oxford was regarded as a triumph for himself and his family. But it may also have caused much resentment because it was an expensive venture. He did not have a Rhodes scholarship, though he had applied for several years. His friend, Hector Wynter, who went to Jamaica College with him, still thinks that race and colour played a big part in spoiling Neville's chances. He was not well enough connected to the power-brokers in Kingston. Neville was a country boy; a brilliant student and a remarkable athlete, but he was too young, and there was always a backlog of good people who were getting too old to apply – and many who got it had no business getting it.

But Neville was determined to go to Oxford and he worked to find the funding and expected to be helped by his family. He was also determined to have some company while there, so he forced Hector Wynter to continue to apply for the Rhodes. Hector was adamant that it was pointless. On the final day for applications, Hector had still done nothing about it. Neville got the forms, filled them out, and then brought them to Hector's home for him to sign. Neville even delivered the application himself. Hector won the scholarship that year. He remembers Neville's elation – no rancour, no regret.

The years in England may have been culturally and intellectually rich, delicious times, but they were also tough financially. I did not understand this at first, seduced as I was by the photographs of him in a crowded bedsit with a gang of his friends, all white, all giddy with the glow of alcohol and laughter in their eyes, wearing strange hats and garish clothes – the world of Oxford. Those seemed like happy times. Then there was that photograph of him strolling through London on an autumn afternoon, in his tweed suit, the trousers billowing around his lithe legs, his jacket pocketing the wind, his face grinning with a familiar sense of well-being. In that photograph, he is walking beside Hector Wynter, lighter skinned, with a moustache, whose more carefully tailored suit – a black get-up with straighter lines and topped with a sharp bow-tie – created a peculiar oddness to their companionship. But they walked through London as if they owned the place. A few years ago, I was walking with a friend along the Thames. We drew our coats tight against our bodies as the musty old smell of the brown river circled around us. And there, in a small park just on the river bank, I saw the photograph again. I saw the exact place, the statue by Rodin in the background, the benches, the cobbled path, the scattering of leaves and the massive oak trees. This time Neville was not in it, but I felt a strong connection to him, to that time. I understood the sense of freedom and yet I understood now the hardship that it had involved. Now, when I recall his breezy clothes, I realize that he was probably quite hungry. Now, I had the hindsight of his letters – the ones we found among his other papers when he died – written in his tidy hand, small, even lettering moving steadily across the pale blue air-letter sheets. Letters addressed to his mother, to his sisters and some to his brother. Often, my father was complaining, like a bit of a brat, about his suffering, about his desperation for money. His sisters helped to keep him at Oxford. One sister, Nellie, until her death, regarded, with a burdensome sense of ownership, my father's Oxford credentials, as hers. The story is that she gave up a very promising opportunity to study medicine so that Neville could finish his degree in English at Oxford. She had kept the tools of surgery in a velvet case as a reminder of what might have been. Neville was the golden boy and he always got taken care of. Flo, the eldest, had to turn to America, where we found her in New York that Spring of 1966. Nellie came to and stayed in England, did Law, but not the medicine she wanted to do.

I don't recall much about the American trip, but there were two notable truths about it. The first was that Neville did not travel with us. At the time, I knew nothing of his vow never to set foot in America, but his absence was not unusual. Neville travelled with us only once in our lives, and that was in the seventies on a trip to England and Ghana. Beyond that, my mother travelled alone with the five of us, even when the entire family was going to the same place. There was one occasion when my mother made all the arrangements for our trip without letting my father know. We were in Ghana. She wanted to take us to Jamaica to meet his family and she knew he would have been hesitant about this. So she planned it single-handedly and, true to her growing position as Mama the Great, embarked on a lengthy journey with four young children in tow. She was barely twenty-six years old. Our journey took us to Jamaica and then on to Guyana where my father was.

The second truth was an incident that would become a part of our defining family myth and that would return to me in strange ways when I considered America as a place of settlement. The story goes that while moving through Kennedy International Airport, we four children, the eldest then eight, marched through the passageways, rollickingly singing the communist anthem, "The Internationale". We knew it quite well; it had been drilled into us by Neville, and along with folk songs, hymns and the songs taught by our grandmother, "The Internationale" was one of the tunes we liked. My father was, with much irony but some clear purpose, cultivating little radicals. I think he would have loved to take credit for orchestrating our little tour-de-force in the Kennedy International, for he relished the moments when he could parade us before his friends. He would order us to lift our knees and swing our arms in exaggerated military fashion while belting out the "Internationale". We enjoyed it greatly, the vigour of the song, the martial exuberance, and the amazement, amusement, and gleeful indulgence of his watching friends. They would laugh and shake their heads, making a mental note for the archives: "This Neville Dawes is a living legend, a character and a half." We had learned well and while no one seemed perturbed by our singing in the middle of the airport, my mother had pulled away from us – far enough to seem like an amazed spectator of this cute display.

Beyond this, America is a blur. But it was now on our list of "places I have been to", a list that, as children, we made with competitive passion. We would count who had been abroad the most, and who had been (we were urban children) to the country the most. We kept this up until our late teens or older. I had pulled ahead of everyone by the second year of university. My trips abroad, separate from the family, had grown to include Guyana, the Dominican Republic, Haiti, the Cayman Islands, and finally, America. My rural list had been nicely beefed up by numerous cadet camps and solo jaunts to the North Coast.

But as Ghana had been, Jamaica, too, was becoming a place of temporary settlement. The sense of always waiting to go somewhere else haunted my father and he passed that on to me.

This condition dictates how you relate to the place in which you live. You learn to observe from a distance. You suspect nationalism, at least the nationalism of the country you are living in. In Ghana, I would say that I was really Jamaican and that I was going to go there to attend Jamaica College, as my father had done. In Jamaica I was Ghanaian. I was different. It was a source of identity and stability. I am not sure I know how to be rooted, totally nationalistic. It is something that fascinates me about America. There is none of that rootlessness, especially in places like Columbia or Sumter, South Carolina. People don't even imagine travelling as particularly interesting or at all necessary for the human condition. Travel, even to another city or another state, is a peculiar thing for many people I talk to. It has to do with an American sense of self-sufficiency,

21

the conviction that nothing out there is better or more interesting than what is here. One can live and die in a small town without having to know of a world beyond that space. This is virtually impossible for even the most remote of Third World peoples because American culture is so insidious, so present, that it seeps into their lives, demanding of them some position about the world beyond their own tiny cosmos.

It makes sense, then, that I would end up in some place other than Ghana or Jamaica. America was unexpected, but it happened. So living here has been about reconciling my memories of my father and his dreams with the pragmatics of my life and the realisation that I had long outgrown those dreams. Yet what he did have was a comfort in movement, and an uncomplicated sense of family and fathering. He had to, however, learn to be the Jamaican father of Ghanaian children for many years. In a sense, I would have to contend with something similar, if more problematic, being the Jamaican/Ghanaian father of Canadian/American children. Just those double-barrelled qualifiers begin to suggest the complications.

CHAPTER 2

passport control

My father left me no nation. It is hard to blame him for this, but it might have made life simpler if he could have offered more sustained concepts of home and nation. I have inherited this absence of home and will now pass it on, in some way, to my children. The facts alone – which I sometimes rehearse to baffle strangers – offer some hints as to why for me "home" is a curious concept. When my children were born, two in Sumter, South Carolina, one in Canada, I realized that at one level they would be calling North America, and perhaps the United States, home. Yet I also felt that they might well be conflicted about home, and one source from whence they would expect to receive their legal and psychic sense of home – their father – would be most unreliable, most unhelpful. This is one inheritance my children entered the world with.

I am Ghanaian. This is my legal label. I was born there. It is my inheritance. My mother is Ghanaian – she was born there and her ancestors came from Togoland and from Ghana. Now anyone listening to me or reading my poetry or fiction would recognize that I am, culturally, largely Jamaican. I grew up in Jamaica. My father was Jamaican and in the early 1970s decided to take his family from Ghana to go and live in Jamaica. This is all simple enough. I am a product of my parents, and, technically, I should have access to both nationalities. But I don't. I tried to have this arranged when, in 1983, I was going to the Dominican Republic to train some fellow students in evangelistic techniques.

I called the Embassy of the Dominican Republic to see if I would need a visa to enter that country. They said I wouldn't. They asked me no questions other than whether I had a passport. I had. I was to travel through Haiti, spending a couple of hours there. It was a late afternoon when I arrived at the congested and hot Port au Prince airport. I joined a line to the customs desk where they examined the papers of those taking the connecting flight to Santo Domingo. That is where the trouble began. I was asked to stand aside. I strained to make sense of a babble of language that jumped from a consonant-free Spanish to a truncated French, to a fluid but utterly incomprehensible patois. I picked up enough to know that my Ghanaian passport was a problem. They asked for my visa. I said I was told I did not need a visa. They asked where I lived. I said Jamaica. They seemed not to believe me. I tried to show from my passport my last record of travel and to prove that I lived in Jamaica. It did not work. There was no permanent resident stamp in my passport. As far as they were concerned, I was a Ghanaian trying to get into the Dominican Republic illegally. They would not let me in. They suggested I get a visa from their embassy in Haiti. The Haitians, of course, were happy to have an African. I loved Haiti for that. But not the Dominicans. Getting a visa was going to be a problem. It was Friday and the following Monday was a public holiday. It was past five in the evening. I was stranded. I spent almost a week in Haiti before I could get the visa. I did my work in Santo Domingo, but it was somewhat marred by this incident. I was annoyed at the inconvenience and disturbed at my abject vulnerability.

Over the years, I came to accept this kind of scrutiny and

suspicion as part of my journey through customs anywhere in the world. When you have a Ghanaian (or Indian, Nigerian, or Bangladeshi) passport, you never feel welcomed at any port. The ritual is one characterized by the assumption of your criminality, of your guilt. You approach the desk with all your papers in order, yet with a sense of being called to prove yourself. You learn to be clear, polite, and efficient, because you recognize that these people have power, all the power. You approach the desk aware that the task before the clerk is to find out why *not* to let you in. The impression is that the country you are entering does not want you there. It is an unreasonable feeling, this very personal feeling of shame, but I have been through enough long interrogations at airports when my papers were in perfect order, to make me declare this ritual of arrival a deeply painful one.

After Haiti and the Dominican Republic, I contemplated being rid of the Ghanaian passport. At least a Jamaican passport would give me access to the Caribbean without problems, and Jamaica, at that time, was not officially blacklisted at most immigration desks. I struggled with this because all through my ten or so years in Jamaica, I had taken pride in being different, in being someone else, being from Ghana. It was, for instance, how I explained my inability to cope with the violence of Jamaican society. In Ghana, that kind of volatile violence – sudden, efficient, and totally inexplicable – was rare. And I did not want to give the Afrophobes in Jamaica – that group of Jamaicans who liked to tell me that despite all their hand-wringing and groaning about slavery and about being torn from "Mother Africa", they were glad it had happened, because they had been rescued from the uncivilized world of that continent to the glorious world of the West. I did not want to give them the pleasure of saying, "See, you too can't stand your Africanness." But I needed some stability. Eventually, I decided to go to the passport office in Kingston and apply for a new passport – a Jamaican passport.

The passport office was on Marcus Garvey Drive, a busy dual carriageway that spilled its load of coughing trucks, ancient vans, road-weary and weighed-down minibuses stuffed to overflowing with passengers, who did not seem to recognize their recklessness in boarding such vehicles that swayed and staggered between the potholes littering the boulevard. Marcus Garvey Drive is flanked by some of the toughest areas in Kingston; "ghetto" is too organized a word for the chaos and squalor of these clotted fields of zinc, cardboard, and timeworn cement where people eke out a living. Riverton City, riverless, a glinting monolith of colour and rust is on Marcus Garvey Drive, along with an assortment of long-established factories: the Tia Maria factory with its exotically shaped gigantic bottle overlooking the road; the soap factory spewing a nauseating chemical stench over everything. The trees and bushes that survived this onslaught of exhaust fumes, stinking chemicals and the relentless sun had an olive green unhealthiness about them; a peculiar dullness of colour that made their very survival seem a mistake.

When you walked along Marcus Garvey Drive, you felt you were quite totally in Jamaica, in a place of violent and complex energy, a place in which hardship was scored to a reggae sound: gritty, unvarnished, and yet miraculous. It was a blazing morning. I caught a bus in Papine, a square nestled at the foot of the Blue Mountains, and continued through Half-Way Tree all the way down to the Three Mile roundabout. I came out onto Marcus Garvey Drive, my body reacting at once to the dust and the stench from the soap factory. I spat. But I was going to get this thing done, this thing that would take an hour at the most, this thing that would secure my status as Jamaican. I was aware that I was giving up something, my uniqueness, the African in me – but I was being pragmatic. I was a New World man, now. I was a writer, a Jamaican writer and that was that.

It never occurred to me that Jamaica would not want me. I had lived in Jamaica for fourteen years. At the time, I had no intention of leaving the country. England was an impossibility – I had no ties there – and America was only for the fickle, the sell-outs, the unpatriotic, the materialistic, the "lickey-lickey", the bourgeois. America was "Mee-ami", the haven for those who valued foreign things over local things. I was overbearingly dogmatic about this. Perhaps I could afford to be because I had no prospect of going to America and I had no desire to do so. I was, at the time, writing my Master's dissertation. After it was done, I planned to go on to do a doctorate, perhaps, and get some teaching work somewhere in the Caribbean. Even if I had been tempted by the idea of getting to America, I was revolted by the thought of going to the American Embassy to join the long line of desperate people looking for escape, to grovel before rude and smug Embassy officials. I was not planning to do this. So since I was going to stay in Jamaica, I might as well legalize my status.

I was confident about my Jamaicanness. I spoke patois. I had been educated there. I had not paid differential fees for school. I had won a national scholarship to its university. I had won national awards as a playwright; reviewers were calling me a Jamaican playwright of promise; there were newspaper clippings to prove all this. I was not just Jamaican, I was making Jamaica proud. I had been called up to the National Youth Cricket trials to represent Jamaica. I did not make the team, but I was at the trials. Everyone knew I was Jamaican. My father was the great Jamaican novelist, and one of the custodians of Jamaican culture in his position as Director of the Institute of Jamaica. People knew him. I could call his name if need be.

The truth is that I did not know anything about what I had to do to get a Jamaican passport. I arrived at the office – a huge hangar-like structure with a zinc roof – with nothing but my Ghanaian passport tucked into my book bag. I did not expect to receive the blue Jamaican passport that day, but I did expect to fill in the forms and get the process started.

27

I was sent upstairs to a darkened floor with a maze of cubicles carved out of this factory-like space. Fans, table fans, whirred. White-shirted, tie-wearing clerks and uncomfortably dressed women in skirt suits sipped iced juices and looked lazily involved with their labours. I found the woman I was to talk to. She wore a dark suit. Her coiffure was helmet-steady, the processing not able to undermine the stern roots of her hair. Her forehead gleamed with sweat and make-up: round lips, fist-like nose, plucked brown eyebrows, efficient gold-earrings.

I explained quickly that I wanted to get a Jamaican passport.

"You ever have one before?" she asked, not looking at me. Slow, noncommittal, very detached.

"No, not a Jamaican," I said.

"But you have a passport, then?" she asked.

"Yes."

"What kind?" She looked at me.

"Ghanaian." I said, taking out the passport.

"Guyanese? So why you want a Jamaican passport, anyway? Don't you have a Guyanese passport already?" She seemed genuinely puzzled by my request.

"Ghanaian. From Ghana." I said.

"Africa?" Her nose curled. "Africa?"

"Yes, West Africa. My Ghana passport has expired and I decided to get a Jamaican one instead." I tried to sound convincingly Jamaican. Her reaction to my Africanness was not a good sign.

"So you are Ghanaian... How do you say it?"

"Ghanaian. Yes," I said.

"Then you must get a Ghana passport. You were born there, right?' It was now as if she was talking to a child. Perhaps I had hoped she would be puzzled by my strong Jamaican accent. I wanted a point of connection, a sense that we were one, that we were Jamaicans together.

"No, but I am Jamaican, too," I said, and then quickly added,

"I have lived here for fourteen years. Went to school here and everything. I am at UWI now. My father is Jamaican."

"Born here?" she asked.

"No. He was born in Nigeria, but he came here when he was two."

"Your mother?"

"But I have lived here for fourteen years ..." For some reason, this was not going as I had planned. I was feeling the urge to pull out my information about scholarships and the like – all the evidence that everyone saw me as Jamaican. Everyone.

"Your mother is Jamaican?" she asked again.

"No. Ghanaian." I said.

"So you are Ghanaian." She said this with a note of triumph, as if she had just won an argument.

" I know..." I stated. She interrupted me.

"And you have not been naturalized?"

"I came for a passport. To get a Jamaican passport..."

Perhaps I caused what happened next. It may have been my sense of being put-upon, it may have been inordinate pride, for all of a sudden, here I was looking like a poor supplicant come to beg something from this country that I had, after much consideration, decided to embrace as my own. I had given up years of feeling almost superior in my Ghanaianness, my difference; I had come to offer my identity to this country and this woman was starting to make me feel as if I was back in the American embassy trying to get a visa. I kept wondering how many people came to her in a year asking to be made a Jamaican. Was she relishing this sense of superiority, that at last a poor African was now seeing how valuable it was to be a Jamaican? Was that what was coming out, or was it all in me, in my shock at being treated as a beggar, my shock at the thought that perhaps the racist poison that I had managed to deflect as a child, with a sense of superiority, was now coming back to haunt me?

Whatever it was, I know I became curt and that the edge in my voice and manner was apparent. It might be juvenile to say it, but she started it. She actually looked at me and laughed, and then quite haughtily (at least so it seemed to me, then), and sternly said:

"You think we just give out Jamaican citizenship like that? You think it so easy? You think we just give it out to any and everybody?" Then she gave that "humph" which was at once amused and impatient. After that, her tone assumed that saccharine civil servant quality of complete lack of interest. "I am sorry, sir, but you can't inherit nationality from your father. He is Jamaican, but naturalized. He could get it from his father, but you can't get it from him because is Nigeria him born. So I can't help you. If you want to naturalize, you going to have to apply for citizenship, and I don't deal with that."

She was finished. I was livid. I had been stupid to have come without finding out any of this, but she did not have to assume that air, that manner. At that moment, I began to rehearse all the things I hated about this little island, this tiny colonial dot of insignificance. I was frustrated by my helplessness, and by the absurdity of the notion that fourteen years in the country did not qualify me for status. I told her that I resented her tone, that I did not come begging for anything, that they could keep their damned passport for all I cared, and I stormed out of the building, my armpits stinging with anger and shame.

So, my father had left us with a confusing heritage, a complicated inheritance. Of course, that last sentence sounds like blame. It really is not. It is a simple observation. But it is one that disturbs me. It implies that the choices parents make about where their children grow up can significantly complicate their lives. When Lorna and I began to have children in North America, whilst expecting to live in Jamaica, a familiar pattern seemed to be recurring. Sena, our eldest, was born in Canada, but I expected to complete my doctorate and return to Jamaica to work. Lorna had already successfully applied for a position at the library of the University of the West Indies, while my application for a post at the Creative Arts Centre was looking promising. Jamaica it would be. True, Sena would be a Canadian child, but this would simply be a bonus, an option for her in later life. We did not plan it that way, but it was something that made sense.

But my Jamaican position fell through and an opportunity came up in America. We decided that, for this first move, the family would follow my job. This meant a complete realignment of our plans. At some levels, the decision to take the position in South Carolina was not a hard one to make. There was the obvious pressure of finances: we wanted more children and so had to start planning for more stability. I needed a job. Our lives during my student years were very difficult financially, and when the scholarship money dried up, I had to work in all kinds of unusual areas to supplement the money Lorna was making as a telemarketer. We were hurting. The band – the reggae band I played with, Ujamaa – was constantly on the verge of a great deal but it did not happen – over and over again. South Carolina was offered and I was surprised at how easily I became drawn to the idea of moving there.

It may have been a reaction to my sense of having been rejected by Jamaica, to my anger at the troubling way Jamaica had dealt with me. Ironically, it was also a response to my father's experience in Jamaica, those dark years of unemployment, of being avoided by the people who once claimed to be his friends, his fall down the stairs in Mandeville after he had accepted a job teaching high school, because he could get nothing else. Those things came back to me, and suddenly taking the job in America seemed like fitting revenge – a lashing out against the affront of his rejection.

I, too, had been rejected and from what I could tell, had fallen victim to one of those insidious Jamaican problems with "connections". The position I had applied for seemed perfectly suited to my experience and abilities. I was assured that I was favoured for the position. But soon, I stopped getting calls from Jamaica asking about my plans to arrive to take up the post. I finally called and was told that someone else had been hired. No one had thought to tell me. I called some friends on the campus and discovered that I had been pushed aside because of a deal with some other person. I did not want to believe this, but it was enough that I had been shafted in a rather rude and unprofessional manner. That was Jamaica for you. I would go to America, go anywhere.

But it would not be simple living in America. Jamaica would remain home, my point of identity. I was not an immigrant in search of a new home, a place to plant roots. I was really a man looking for work. I was, then, a typical Caribbean immigrant seeking a better livelihood. But moving to America would immediately force me to re-evaluate my aversion to America and its consuming culture, particularly as we negotiated the challenge of raising American-born children. We had to learn how to teach about patriotism and nationalism in a society whose nationalism did not always appeal to us. Above all, I had to cope with the legacy of my father's attitude to America which had so shaped my own. All of this was complicated by the fact that we were going to live in a part of America that had no thriving West Indian community or a notable tradition of West Indian immigration beyond the exchange of slaves that occurred in the eighteenth and early nineteenth centuries between Barbados and Charleston, and the occasional migrant farm workers who littered the peach farms around the state.

The race problems of South Carolina were not unknown to me. I did, indeed, ask about those things when I was being interviewed for the position. This was the Deep South, a place I had read about and developed a whole range of ideas about: a tough world with a history of race problems that I would have to come to terms with. We knew no one in South Carolina. We were starting from scratch. This journey, which continues, has forced me to revisit the memory of my other varied journeys and, especially, the journeys of my father as an immigrant.

I come from a family that has travelled much. My Jamaican great-grandparents were the descendants of a mixture of slaves and Anglo/Irish immigrants to Jamaica. My father's parents spent much of their adult lives as immigrant missionaries in Nigeria, where my father was born. My father continued this pattern by journeying to Ghana from Jamaica to live as an immigrant and to marry a Ghanaian there. I was born in Ghana, grew up in Jamaica and London and was now facing America as another port of call. Kamau Brathwaite's "pathless, harbourless spade" described us exactly. And that was just my side of the family. Lorna's family had travelled too. From Jamaica to Panama then back to Jamaica and then to England on her mother's side. Lorna was born in London and found herself an alien in Kingston when she moved there a year before I did. We were used to moving, to the shifting of landscapes, to the different tastes of food, to thinking of relatives as being somewhere else. And here we were, introducing our children to this tradition of uprooting, moving, journeying.

When we arrived in Sumter, South Carolina, in the fall of 1992, we were starting afresh. Sena was just over seven months old. Lorna and I had been married for two years. This was my first full-time job and everything was new. Sumter was still recovering from the ravages of hurricane Hugo, yet the flaming of fall leaves was apparent all around. It was hard to take in the landscape, though, preoccupied as we were by the business of settling down: getting a social security card, getting a bank account, arranging payment schedules at work, finding an apartment, finding furniture, finding the nearest supermarket, discovering the impracticality of being carless, and finding our bodies and minds constantly anxious about racism, its legacy and its presence. We were trying to assess the meaning of difference in this new world: where could we go or not go? These issues would consume us during those early days. As we contended with the basic details of settling, we could tell that we had much to learn about living in America. And yet America did not seem alien to us. We could recognize most things about the society. By the time we had our television installed, we were abreast of the basic details of the American world. Canada is not far from America and it represents an excellent point of transition. The superficial details of American life are present in Canada – what is on television is virtually the same and the news is cluttered with American items – and the differences are often so slight that they seem like nuanced versions of the same thing. So it was not hard to say that we knew this society quite well before we got there. What we were not prepared for was the more difficult business of race in the South. I am not talking about racism, *per se*, but the mere fact that we were now in a society with its own distinctive racial make-up. Jamaica was predominantly black. Canada was predominantly white and blackness in Canada was typically immigrant based. South Carolina was very black – more blacks than we had seen in one place since Jamaica – and yet it was also quite decidedly a white-run society. This was far more complicated. Blackness in America was American, not foreign, not immigrant. This introduced other complications of race and politics. America was new in that sense. Years of watching American television could not prepare you properly for the distinct history and present of South Carolina. Popular American culture painted a picture of the South that was marked by cliché and hyperbole. I had to relearn a great deal.

We lived in a small apartment, spending nights on our makeshift bed – a pile of thick blankets laid out on the carpeted floor. We spent our time counting the dollars, waiting for the first pay check and wondering what would become of us in this new place – what new friends we would make and what new lives we would find here.

It was not my first time in America nor was it Lorna's. She had been to Chicago to visit her sister a few times in the past. I had been in America several months before during the intensive interview process. Before that I had made several extended excursions into this country. But this was different. Now I was entering as a permanent resident; I was going to be living indefinitely in America. Now, I was living in what could be called unequivocally "the Deep South", "the Bible Belt", the "Heart of the Confederacy", "Dixie". The Confederate flag flew atop the state legislature in the capital. Now the question of nation would be thrown into relief. Defining home would be increasingly important in the face of the overwhelming force of American culture. The legacy of my parents, particularly my father, would now be tested. I had no idea how it would all work out.

CHAPTER 3

resisting the anomie

Before that 1992 arrival, whenever I had toyed with the notion of living in America, I had regarded the idea as abhorrent. It was not merely a case of liking or disliking America as a place to be, because by the end of my six-month stay in America in 1986, I could envisage liking aspects of this place. But I still had much of my father's monumental aversion to America as a political entity, and this went along with my own instinctive, unreasoned, but deeply defining attitudes that made the idea of living in America an act of betrayal – a betrayal of the Third World, a betrayal of my conviction that there were worlds outside America that were much more pleasant and endearing. America meant a materialistic approach to life and that was inimical, I thought, to who I was and what I wanted to be. I had long had the self-righteousness, which was also a profound kind of idealism, that made me aggressive towards the kind of American evangelist who came to Jamaica to bring the *real* truth of Christ to the Third World. I really had no patience with them. I did not listen to American evangelists on television or read American Christian scholars because they were, as far as I was concerned, part and parcel of the imperialist pattern. I really did speak like that too. It was rhetoric, but sincere and passionate rhetoric. I was in that mode when I came to America in 1986, and that period really confirmed much of what I felt about America – even as it started to challenge my views.

In Lincoln, Nebraska, sometime in November 1986, I was a beleaguered man. The crowd in the auditorium in which I stood – full of high-school seniors, all white and apparently the brightest of the state – was hostile. I had no idea that American patriotism was so intense among such young people. But then, those were the Reagan years, the years when Americans felt put upon by the ingratitude of other nations who seemed to forget that American "intervention" was for their own good. This was in the aftermath of the invasion of Grenada, that absurd and outrageous "rescue" effort which showed America to be most thug-like in manner. I had said this to this gathering of students, this and other things, and they were hopping mad.

"Well, if you dislike this country so much, why don't you go home?" one student shouted.

"You all come here to benefit from America's wealth and then crap all over us," another offered.

"Why do you live here, then?"

I faced these attitudes with a smug calm. I enjoyed the idea that I was here in America at the invitation of the American government. That was true. I was twenty-four and a young playwright who had somehow gained enough attention to be recommended for the attractive International Writers Program sponsored by the University of Iowa and the United States Information Service. I would, along with forty other important writers from thirty-eight different countries, spend half a year in America, writing, teaching, giving readings and lectures, seeing the country and meeting people.

This Lincoln trip was one I agreed to at the last minute. They needed three people from the program to go to Lincoln to talk to these students about how America was viewed by the rest of the world. The congressman who was hosting the event, and who wrote to us on very official-looking congressional stationery, wanted us to be candid, to be direct and to pull no punches.

The other two who agreed to go were Edwin Thumbo and Inkeri Kilpernin. Thumbo is a distinguished poet from Singapore – a mature man with a rumbling manner, brusque and confident, but with a capacity to be witty and charming. I always felt uncomfortable calling him Edwin – I wanted to call him Professor Thumbo or sir, for he struck me as a typical university professor who had emerged out of the very British commonwealth tradition. He knew America. He had been here before on many occasions. He would talk about America and Singapore. Inkeri Kilpernin is a Finnish playwright, a grandmotherly woman whose plays startled me with their un-grandmotherly daring. She smiled a great deal and was enjoying her visit to America tremendously. In some ways, I was under her wing as she encouraged me to shift from the overly religious themes in my work and focus on sexuality, class, racial tension, and so on. I was not quite buying any of it (after all, I had to resist all efforts to dampen my Christian ardour), but I was charmed by her interest. She would talk about America and her country. It was left to me to talk about the rest of the world, I felt.

I had not planned to be offensive. I had planned, in fact, to speak honestly about how impressed I had been with the wealth of knowledge available in America, in its museums, libraries, archives, and on computerised databases. I wanted to talk about the size of the nation and the admirable progress it had made in only two hundred or so years. I planned to talk about the influence of American music on World music and the powerful impact that Black history and experience in America had had on Africa and the Caribbean over the last hundred and fifty years. It was all going to be positive and, I expected, informative.

We had discussed the order of the presentations as we walked across a flaming orange courtyard strewn with fallen leaves and framed by a stand of white-barked trees that glowed sharply against the ashen sky. The campus was on a hillside and the wind was especially vicious, blowing off the acres and acres of corn fields that stretched all around this tiny bluff. I was to talk last; Inkeri would go first.

This is perhaps what led to the carnage that followed. Inkeri was determined to use the talk to thank the US for their entry into her country when she was a child. She almost wept as she recalled the aftermath of the Second World War and America's liberating march. In her mind, they did not have to intervene and she remembered with nostalgia and deep fondness the gum-chewing GI's who represented freedom and peace. She admonished the students to take pride in their nation, a great nation that had made a tremendous difference to her life. I was already beginning to sense that the burden of ruthless candour was going to fall on me. I had taken the congressman's instructions to heart. In retrospect, I suspect that we were asked to do this talk because he perceived us to be already compromised into gratitude to America, if not with a sense of loyalty. The USIS was putting good money into this program, one that was quite blatantly described to us as aimed at ameliorating the negative image of America that existed abroad. They were keen on getting writers to write about America after the trip, to write in ways that would aid America's image. I listened to all this, at first with some alarm. Had I been co-opted, duped into this by my overweening sense of pride at being selected and by the quite remarkable way a visa was secured for me without my having to step into the demoralizing dark hole of the U.S. Embassy's basement? There Jamaicans sat sweating, like chained denizens of a slave ship, waiting desperately for a visa to freedom. So far, the congressman was *not* getting what he wanted. Inkeri thanked the USIS and the University of Iowa for allowing her to come to America to say thank you, to say that for her America was a very dear country.

39

Edwin Thumbo seemed to have been caught up in the spirit of diplomatic goodwill that Inkeri had started and he forgot everything about American encroachment on the sovereignty of countries in Southeast Asia, forgot the Vietnam War, forgot the Philippines; forgot it all. He was eloquent in his tale about the influence of American economics, American capital in shaping the economy of Singapore and transforming it into something powerful. America was a place of greatness and promise and people looked to it for these things.

I looked at the congressman. He was beaming, but I imagined he was really disappointed by this saccharine presentation. I also sensed something far more compelling stirring inside me. America was not such an innocent and most people who lived outside America did so because they wanted to and not because, as some Americans think, they could not get into America. I grew up in Ghana in the 1960s and in Jamaica in the 1970s; America was not the golden boy of wonder or beauty for me. American culture was pervasive, but its impact was not always positive at all. There were people all over the world who hated America, who thought of America as a crassly materialistic Hollywood set. These well-scrubbed white Nebraskans needed to know this. So after Edwin sat down to warm applause, I told them as much.

I thought the congressman, at least, would be pleased, but in truth, I was past caring about that. Mine was an anti-American excursion: rough, explicit in detail, quite clearly painful and, in retrospect, imprudent. I looked at Edwin and Inkeri; Edwin was grimacing, hoping it would look like a smile, while Inkeri was looking down, her body all flushed. It did not take them long to distance themselves from my diatribe when the first barrage of questions came. Inkeri smiled sweetly and spoke of me as a hot-headed child from a hot-headed society who had not truly understood the value of American intervention. Edwin was more generous, offering that some did hold very negative views about America, but it was important to celebrate the fact that others, himself included, appreciated the pressure America was under to be a world leader. His anti-Russian position was not subtle. I avoided a debate with either of them; I was too busy fielding the questions about my person, my motives, my immigration status.

I was proud that I had no intention of staying in America. That was genuine. Nothing I had seen, nothing I had heard during the months I had so far spent in that country had swayed me from thinking that I would never live in America. I had signed the proviso that as a holder of the special visa to be a part of this program, I would be barred from entry into the US for two years after the program, without regret or uncertainty. I had no plans to return. I was blunt.

"You people have this notion that everyone in the world would die to live in America. You assume this. But it is wrong. I don't plan to live here. I was invited here by your government," I said. The questions grew more combative.

"But I was living in India as a student and my friend in the US embassy said people would do anything to come here..." a girl shouted.

"You think it is because they adore America, because they believe in your foreign policies, because they believe in America's system of government? Not really. They see money in America. They want some of it. People don't always come here because they admire America. And you should not expect them to. Look at you, all angry and ready to gang up on me because I, this black foreigner, have said bad things about America when my stomach is full of the tasty pastries provided by your congressman with your tax dollars. That pisses you off, doesn't it? But it is a reality you must face. I have a right to hold this view and you should let me do so..."

It was easy for me then. Later it was not so easy. I became a permanent resident. I had a green card. Of course, no one asked me to give such speeches any more, but the pressure to conform to America's expectations of immigrants was far more intense. You surrender something when you decide to be an immigrant, when you choose to settle in a new country. All the rituals surrounding immigration make you a beggar, a petitioner, the one who wants something, the one who, ultimately, must be grateful. Every time I returned to America from abroad, I was made acutely aware of this. Immigration desks still involve a rite of arrival that remind me of my alienness. I cannot imagine what it is like to approach an immigration agent with nonchalance. For many people, I am sure, immigration desks are merely brief inconveniences because of the long line. They slip their American passports onto the desk, collect it at once, accept the "Welcome home", and move on. No anxiety, no paranoia about being pulled to one side, no long wait while the computer searches out your name; no sense that this time, this time they will simply say "no". That is the life of the immigrant when entry into the country is predicated on the principle of petition. You beg; they give.

My green card: I was supposed to recognise that it was given to me; it was a gift, an act of kindness by the government. This despite the fact that my family spent a thousand dollars to get our cards. This despite the fact that I was invited here to work, presumably because it was felt that America could use me. Indeed, once I had accepted the post, I was *instructed* to arrive by a certain date. Somehow, the equation was altered when I needed to get a green card. I was the one who had to prove my worthiness and I had to be grateful to those who gave me the card. It is not that I find this inherently wrong. Hardly. It is the way of the world. But what bothers me is the way it can make you feel. It has left me feeling compromised, forced to acknowledge a connection to this country, a connection that wants to deny me the freedom of difference, the freedom to be dispassionately critical. This is the comfort of marginality – it's far easier to attack the centre from the margins because nothing is compromised in the margins. Once you enter the centre, you are invariably compromised. I miss that marginal space.

In this new space, I had to think of myself as living in America and having to construct a meaningful life here. My children were going to have to contend with being insiders, part of the fabric, and I would, by extension, have to cope with that. This was a new condition for me and it was the closest thing to feeling quite rootless. It was not that home was hard to conceive, for I had ways of imagining a home outside of this society. Yet I also suspected that South Carolina was becoming home and the meaning of this new "home" was part of what made it all hard to define.

To cope with loneliness and the encroachment of despair caused by homesickness, to cope with the sense of alienation that overtook me on a much anticipated return to Jamaica in 1997, some five years after my last visit. I tried to convince myself that home had nothing to do with geography, with nations, that home was where you were, where you decided to name home. In Jamaica, I had, of course, found that the world had marched ahead of me – my friends, my understanding of Kingston's streets, the body language, the feel of sweat on the skin, the state of Jamaican cricket, the shifts in language, the new DJs, musicians, and styles.

This is the immigrant's dilemma: to settle both physically and emotionally in a new place, or to give a halfhearted emotional commitment to settling and, at the same time, to construct an elaborate myth of return. The immigrant who has a home far away is protected from the pressure of always having to say good things about America, the kind of pressure that says simply, "Well, if you hate it so much, what are you doing here?" The immigrant who knows that home is elsewhere can feel some sense of exiled dignity, knows that he or she is more than a rootless nomad, a creature without traditions, without a people. But we also know that the "elsewhere" becomes a fiction, albeit a compelling fiction that evokes the most powerful kind of nostalgia.

This business of rootlessness is real. Why do I still feel a deep-seated need to hold onto my Ghanaian passport when I have not been in that country for almost thirty years? Why do I still refer to Jamaica as home when I have no physical home there? I own a home in America. I own a piece of South Carolina; I own nothing in Ghana or Jamaica. So why does it still bother me that I never did get that Jamaican passport? I have concluded that it has to do with death. Death and the sense that others, connected to you by blood, have walked on the earth that you call home.

I still remember a trip that we took with my father to Sturge Town in St. Ann's many years ago. It was our first time to this place where my father grew up. He drove up the narrow winding roads, the corners sharp and treacherous, looking over into dense mountain vegetation that went deep and dark. He named each corner, pointing to the cluster of trees that gave them their names. He was travelling back and we were imagining the memory with him. Sturge Town was then still so rural that it did not require much imagination to envisage what it would have been like forty years before. Through the trees he pointed to the house, a large building settled into a gently sloping hill's face, a handsome old building with several overhanging porches with ornately carved wooden trimmings. The vegetation around the house was so thick it greened everything: the weather-worn wood, the side walls of old mortar – everything greened with age, as if the house itself had long roots boring down into the mountainside. He took us to the back of the house where the sloped concrete squares where pimento was dried in the sun were cracked and filled with craters. The people living in the house still used it to sun the pimento as my father's family had done for over a century. Above the barbecue area was the ancient frame of the Baptist Church, probably built when Sturge Town was established as one of the first Free Villages founded by ex-slaves and missionaries in 1838. It was in this Church, we imagined, that my father sang parodies of hymns:

Hark the herald angels sing,
Beechams pills are just the thing
Peace on Earth and mercy mild
Two for adults one for child.

I inflated all his stories in my imagination. The song was probably a schoolboy travesty enacted while he was at high school in Kingston, but I imagined it in this church where light beamed through the wooden structure. It was in this church that I placed one of my father's stories about Jamaica, which were almost always fictional tales, but which I somehow took to be true. It was the story of an old, poor woman in the village who one day could not find clothes to wear to church. All she had were the tattered and worn clothes she used in the fields. But she was determined to worship the Lord regardless. I could see her walking up the path by the barbecue squares and entering the church of brilliant light. As she entered, the story went, the church was just getting into stride with the song "Holy, Holy, Holy..." This woman was offended and shouted out to the congregation: "Yes, yes, it holey-holey, but it clean." My father may have had to explain the pun, the Jamaicanism of calling tattered clothes "holey-holey", but the joke would send us into stitches every time, and for me, it located the church in a very solid way.

Deep inside the thick forest near the house, the old trees rose to dizzying heights and the dense canopy made everything cool, the path dense and soft. Crowded with untamed bushes,

45

weeds and wild flowers were the gravestones of stained cement that marked the resting places of my grandfather and great grandmother. My blood was buried here. It was moving to imagine this as it somehow made tangible my connection to this place. I could smell death, smell its stark reality and the permanence of history, of memory. It was strange. It was clearly not a traditional family plot. My father's mother was not buried there, nor was my uncle, my father's brother. My father, when he died, should have been, I suppose, but we could not afford it. And there was by then an unalterable contradiction between our personal attachment to this plot of land and the real connection of ownership and commerce. But it is the former that seals that landscape as home. I have a sense that, were I to be buried in Jamaica, I would be cared for by those who had gone before, my flesh and blood.

This mythic conviction is amusing, for it runs counter to what I believe as a Christian. I have never felt myself to be a divided colonial traversing the worlds of Christian belief and belief in the ancestors. There has never been a tension, never been a conversion from Ogun to Christ. Yet I understand the value of the ancestors in the quest for home; it is a natural part of how I view the world, how I view myself. My father's Marxism made faith in Christ an unlikely accommodation. And he was quite sacrilegious about Christianity and sincerely panicked when it was clear that I had become a Christian. When asked about belief, he was cryptic: "J. Christ Esquire, I have never met; but the ancestors, I believe, walk under the earth." He said that if he had to believe in anything spiritual, anything beyond the material realities of this world, it would have to be in the ancestors. He was choosing Africa over Europe. It was easy for us to rationalize this assertion as part and parcel of his anti-imperialist, Pan-Africanist rhetoric, a decision not founded on the absence of Christian faith so much as on ideological considerations. Yet, it was hard to dismiss it all as the ranting of an ideologue. When he said it, he was smiling, but he had thought it through carefully. More troubling for me, I understood the inextricable link that exists between political ideology and faith. I understood this in my home life during my childhood and youth where everything had to be tested along the lines of ideology. For me to believe in Christ, I had to believe that Christianity, at its most essential, did not condone slavery, did not condone oppression and was at odds with the history of subjugation and exploitation that came with the Christian Church over the years. That was my crisis of faith. Neville was speaking in that same context and telling us that he was placing his faith in Africa – the ancestors, blackness – and not in Europe and whiteness.

My father's position was unsettling for me when I became a Christian, for I feared an eternal separation from this man I loved. I had somehow reconciled myself to the validity of Christianity and the notion that it was not an inherently colonial faith. What I was still struggling with was the position of other religions and belief systems – like those of my ancestors. Where did they stand? I had no clear answers, and that uncertainty was what made me worry for Neville after he died. I had made a gamble and hedged my bets. If I was wrong about Christianity, the most I would receive as punishment from my ancestors would be a stern reprimand, but they would welcome me – blood is like that. To reject Christianity and discover it to be the truth would be a terrible thing to do – hell and damnation awaited.

We must have been watching my father's attitude to Christianity closely during the months before his accidental death; the ritual of people who were each probably praying privately, but with fervour, for his soul. We – those of my siblings who claimed Christianity as their faith – shared notes after his death, asking the difficult question about what we thought might have been the nature of his belief in those last months.

It was fascinating to note that all three of us (my two sisters and I) had observed him listening to Christian radio programmes late into the night. We remembered, with a combination of abiding sadness and strange and hopeful assurance, an afternoon when, for the first time in a while, we were all together. It was a Sunday and we had eaten dinner at my sister's apartment in Constant Spring. We indulged the family ritual of singing into the tape recorder (a ritual started by my father in Ghana when he would record his poems and our songs) songs we had learned as children from my mother and her mother, songs my father had taught us and a strange miscellany of popular songs that we enjoyed singing – including a corny collection of Jim Reeves's songs and rather sloppy R&B tunes. My sister would harmonize on Gospel songs –

> *We've come this far by faith*
> *Leaning on the Lord*
> *Trusting in His holy Word*
> *He's never failed us yet...*

– while my youngest brother would wail away on his own compositions. In the apartment that day there was the strain of a family wearied by my brother's antics, his threatening enigma. His eyes flashed from a state of clear-mindedness to a strange paranoia. My mother's face showed her unreasonable guilt and sadness. She was tired. And my father looked smaller than ever, defeated by this burden, by his joblessness, by the fact that it was close to Christmas and it would be impossible to have our typical Christmas at home, because there was no home any more. The conviction of his Marxist faith ("Marxists do not buy houses; we will rent.") had come back to haunt us, to laugh at us, and it was clear that he felt inadequate, as if he had failed. The daily flow of letters of rejection and regret from his many job applications had taken a serious toll. But we sang. We sang with vigour, straining towards an old warmth, a memory of another time that was carefree, filled with uncanny faith and hope. We sang.

Then Aba suggested that we close the visit with prayer. It was a peculiar moment that in an awkward and uncomfortable way suggested the diminishing of my father's power, of his magic, of his dream. It was Aba's apartment, and we, the children, were now the adults in charge. This call to prayer meant that something had changed. My mother always demanded prayer of us; before trips, before examinations, during sicknesses, she would encourage us to pray, to read the psalms, to seek a divine presence. But this was different. It was Aba's idea and she would lead us in a circle of prayer. Everyone prayed. Kojo, the eldest, who claimed a nominal faith, prayed politely as if addressing a chair. Kojovi prayed with fervour, his language swooping through a surreal wave of images, memories, and a desperate need to connect with something beyond himself. Then there was a long silence. No one expected Neville to pray, but it would have been impolite to simply act on this assumption. Maybe it was the pressure of the circle, the silence, or perhaps something more profound – perhaps a spiritual cloud in the place making his participation inevitable.

He spoke calmly as if making an incantation. He did not name the name of the spirit of his choice, the divine. His words came with the simplicity of a blessing – a kind of generic grace that was as essential as a poem. What he said was something of a call for blessing that was intensely prayerful, as if he was aware of his helplessness, his need for something outside himself to work. He prayed as a father. "Help us," he pleaded, "help us to live, help us to stay together, help Kojovi, help Aba, help us to live, help us." I cried. I had no good reason to cry, but I did, for it was a day of strange sadness and yet inexplicable hope. And the three of us who were quite determinedly the "born-agains" had stored that day as one that showed Neville's willingness to look quietly to God. Perhaps he was recalling,

49

we said, some time in his youth when the Baptist church on the hill in Sturge Town fed him with the basic Gospel of faith, the simple catechisms of belief, the hymns of redemption. Perhaps there had once been a time when he had allowed the Spirit to stir in him a faith beyond himself. We felt that maybe it was some such memory that had taken him, drawn him to pray as he did. Or perhaps it was his strong belief in family, in the importance of communal power that he saw as more important than quibbling over issues of faith. Maybe he just respected us, respected his children enough to know what was important to us, and to share that reverence. My father was like that; he did love us a great deal. He defined himself around his family. I think he loved his family far more than anything else he did – writing, his politics, his friends, cricket, books, helping other writers, becoming the foremost cultural critic in the society. He loved his family enough to find it a useful explanation for his lack of creative production. He never showed any bitterness about that – about the fact that it was his mother's impending death that made him leave what was a comfortable and productive world in Ghana to come back to the difficult politics of Jamaica; no bitterness about the fact that he worked where he worked because he had a family to support and the business of being a writer or a scholar would not pay the bills.

I would prefer to believe that it was out of love and respect for his family, (more even than to believe that he was coming into some spiritual revelation) than to believe that he joined us in prayer as an act of defeat or weakness – the weakness of the old and helpless. In truth, he was only fifty-five, but there was a fatigue that gripped him after he lost his job, and I think that he started to believe that he was now old. He walked with a slow resignation to pain and discomfort, carried everything like a burden. My mother would tell him that he was behaving like an old man. He would find it quite funny. In his own mind, he still probably felt like the poet – the romantic poet – who

50

like Dylan Thomas or Shelley, burnt out quickly and gloriously. Those who lived on were marking time, merely pretending an existence. He carried a tragic air with him during those days and, despite my wish that it were not so, it still lingers in my mind that maybe it was his resignation to that feeling, to his sense of impending death, that made him pray with us. When I read Derek Walcott's *The Bounty*, I tend to think of my father. I think of the pleasure in reflection that Walcott has, but I also think of his voice as carrying intimations of death, of dying and the slow fading of the individual artist in the face of an unforgiving history. My father may have paced out countless Walcottian lyrics in his head during those days. His prayer was such a lyric – at once sad, and at the same time, strangely hopeful.

He intoned "Amen," and we joined him with reverence and relief. When our eyes were open, the world was the same: the prospect of our nights in separate places – the family apart, yet striving to stay together.

Yet it was oddly comforting when, on the night after my father's funeral, my Uncle Kofi, dressed in his kente cloth, walked away from the gathering of Ghanaians who had come to pay their respects. I watched him walk barefoot through the grass. It was past midnight and the rum was dwindling. Talk of my father was intense and interspersed with laughter, and the refrain, "Why, Neville, why?" Uncle Kofi, Kofi Awoonor, the poet, who had been a close friend and protégé of my father, became a shadow in the yard. If he had not taken the bottle of rum, one could have assumed he was going aside to take a piss. The talk continued quietly. I kept looking into the dark, to see him, to understand the meaning of the soft incantations in Ewe floating thinly in the air. He came back with his cloth wrapped about his waist, his chest bare, his eyes ablaze and yet strangely at peace.

"He has gone now," he said. They nodded their agreement. They drank more rum and my mother's eyes watered for the comfort of the news and for the presence of these Ghanaians who, it turned out, were Neville's closest and truest friends. They knew how to send him off, they and not his Jamaican friends; they might have failed to invoke the pure logic of the ancestors, as these Ghanaians did. I was comforted because I could picture my father walking along a darkened path, recrossing that Middle Passage, a stretch of sea he had crossed and recrossed in the process of defining home, a stretch of sea so resonant for him it is impossible to explain. I saw him finding his way along these paths, to be met by his ancestors with some rum and water to quench his thirst, to comfort him, to be company for him. I wanted so much for this to be true, for there to be love waiting for him because I knew how much he loved us, how much he loved my mother, how much it all meant to him, being a father, all the gatherings, the ritual of lining us up and counting, then announcing: "My children, my poems." I knew all this and I felt that he would be so alone in death, so deeply alone. This message from my uncle touched me; it touched me the more because he said he had talked to my father there in the Kingston night, and that my father was well, was at peace, was well looked after, and loved us still.

It was the kind of death that brings with it the force of premonition and haunting. The death I foresaw late one night on my way home from a rehearsal of one my plays. I was walking through the residential Mona area, a sprawling suburban development built around the university where university professors and teachers from the schools in the area lived. This was my usual route home, through the strange, un-gridded labyrinth of avenues named after Jamaican flowers, searching out the streets with lights on them, and avoiding the unlit ones with unchained dogs that would leap the fence and attack. I walked the streets quickly, trembling both at the prospect of being attacked by predator gunmen and being confronted by ghosts, spirits of the dark. I walk dark streets in America, even rural America, and I have no fear of spirits because I have no language for the spiritual realm in America. I am sure they are here, too, sure that they lurk in the shadows watching me pass foolishly by, but they don't threaten me because their smell does not seem to carry to me. I have no fear of the undead in these parts. But on one of those walks, I had a vision of my father coming into a darkened theatre, looking at me and then walking away, to climb into a black taxi. The taxi drove off and I had a sense that he was leaving for good, that he was dying. He was alive at the time but I felt an overwhelming sense of foreboding. I got home and wrote a poem about it, filled with fear that I was somehow speaking into being something that I just did not want to happen. When he died within that year, I came to regard the poem and the vision as a haunting, a preparation for loss.

Here in America I have no hauntings. Not like the hauntings I lived with in Jamaica. These made me thrust my penis out of the louvre windows of my bedroom and let flow an arc of urine into the garden late at night because I was too afraid to walk into the dark hall that separated my bedroom from the bathroom. I did not fear anything other than ghosts – ghosts that seemed completely incapable of entering the safe world of my room. This was in urban Kingston, mind you. Yet they were there. The hauntings were strangely intense when my father died. Like the giant moth that took up residence in my office the day after his death. This moth would not leave, no matter what I did. I used a broom and brushed it out of the room. I shut the door and felt satisfied that it was gone. The next morning, it would be in the corner again. It had flown in through the louvres over the door. I could not close the louvres. I was tempted to kill the thing, but a friend warned me against that. He said that it was quite clearly my father coming to visit me for a while before his journey home. I did not buy this, but I found a strange attraction in the notion. I found that the presence of the moth brought me some peace of mind, and I was comforted by the myth. I was so at ease with the moth that I sometimes talked to it. I tend to mutter to myself when I am working on some difficult passage of writing or trying to work my way through a complex idea. I would direct my talks to this moth, exploring the nuances of Plato's ideas, or trying to make sense of Kamau Brathwaite's verse. I referred to the moth as Neville. It was my way of coping, but I did not feel like someone imposing therapy on himself. I was at ease with this surrogate father in my room. I introduced it to visitors who thought it rather a sick kind of joke and some felt that I was clearly not coping well with my father's death. When the moth suddenly disappeared, I missed it. I had to cope with its absence by constructing a myth about its role as a source of assurance for me. In my head, Neville was now somewhere in Ghana, meeting the ancestors.

I am not superstitious. My Christian faith makes superstition an unhelpful proposition. Yet, I sometimes find myself acting out a series of rituals that have to do with a faith beyond my orthodox Christianity. I do not offer this as an articulation of that Walcottian figure "divided to the vein" or the Achebe-esque Nigerian moving from the shrine of the ancestors to the altar of Christ. It is a tempting notion to suggest that I am divided in that way, but I am not, because I recognize that such a divide is a romantic notion that does not really affect the everyday dynamics of my life. But I do know that I carry in me ideas about my father's passing that are beyond my comprehension. If he had died comfortably ensconced in Christian belief, this whole period of questioning and constructing a world beyond his death would not have been part of my thinking. But he did not, and the spiritual world of the earth, the ancestors and all that, is part of my way of contending with his dying. In Jamaica, even with its thoroughly modern realities, there is a tactile, almost electric spiritual dynamic in the air. I think of death in Jamaica and I think of the songs of mourning; I think of white rum and nine nights; I think of the long journey to the grave-site somewhere just outside the city; I think of the drive home at night, the air smelling of death and the dying; I think of the unfurling of my stomach, that strange discomfort that comes with the scent of death and the prospect of death. There, death goes beyond the mere hurting of the heart. It is grounded in the landscape – a grounding not unlike the hauntings I felt in Ghana, those tremblings that made me see nightmares while I listened to the drumming coming from Achimota, carrying the lamentation of people burying their dead. These hauntings were tied to the stories that my mother would tell of old market ladies who would stop her in the market, draw her aside and prophesy, with incredible accuracy, things about her life – and not ask for a penny in recompense. She told those stories not as a catechism of belief, but as a way of accounting for the strangeness of life. I carry those stories in me. They have to do with the meaning of death, the feel of death.

In Jamaica or Ghana, death is tangible, messy, never tidy or efficient, never free of powerful emotions. Death has the scent of rum soaking the earth. Death is a scraggly grave-site in Cape Coast, littered with tall cassava trees and shrubbery, the place where my grandmother is buried. It is a place that smells of kerosene and the Vicks Vapor Rub that filled my nostrils when we spent the night with our aunt, as my mother and her sisters talked in Fanti, recalling their mother – the litany of death.

It is death that roots me to a landscape. I can't imagine my death, my burial, my long walks to a familiar face other than in Jamaica or Ghana. I still struggle with the idea of a death in South Carolina, and this has been an essential part of my feeling of unbelonging in America. My roots here are only modest, like the thin, short roots of the sod turf we planted in the backyard of our first house ten years ago. We sweated to bed it into the soil and watched as the turf greened and took firm rooting. Our neighbours suddenly became quite respectful. Some started to ask us for tips on how to care for sod. We had become experts at this thing. It was almost as if, by planting something in that ground, we had become connected to the people in the area, as if we had shown our willingness to stay, to try and make something of the place. They started to gossip with us and tell horror stories about the last owners of the house. We were in. But for me, this planting had a more tenuous hold.

The truth is that to become truly settled as an immigrant, you have to forget where you are coming from. I was not prepared to do that. And though, at times, I was becoming able to imagine this place as home in that profound and spiritual sense, I knew that it would take more than a new passport and more than the confession of loyalty to this nation in some tiny courtroom. I am still reluctant to even consider being an American. There are conveniences but are they enough? I could be pragmatic and rationalize the move, but it is still difficult for me to do this, even to think about it. Is it that I simply don't believe in this country, believe in the myth of its patriotism? Is it because I cannot honestly claim to own this landscape, to have invested in it with blood? African-Americans are American because they have given everything to this place that has so hated them, so hurt them. But it is their legacy. The earth has taken their blood and, through some remarkable alchemy, created the richness of culture and cultural meaning that is so remarkable in the annals of human history. I am an alien to that legacy even as I admire it and benefit from it.

Of course, there are so many different immigrant experiences and they have a lot to do with where one settles. South Carolina is an old state, without the long and ongoing tradition of immigrant enclaves of places such as New York and Miami. Here the sense of being alien is perhaps of a deeper kind.

Since I have been in South Carolina, I have made a number

of close friends. It is almost a ritual act of friendship for them to routinely invite me to their family reunions. I have had many such invitations. My friend Lana had her family over from all over the country and she wanted me to meet them, to see how they lived, to hear them talk about the past, to eat food and to be a part of the Black family in the south. I declined. I was not sure I could handle being an outsider in such a setting. I declined offers from Gwen, our children's first piano teacher, who invited me to a grand celebration of her mother's birthday. I asked for a report of the event from Lana, who went. She told of family members from all over the country coming to visit and to celebrate. She told of the strange and involved stories they all carried. But it was all family, all a definition of itself, and I knew from those reports that I would have felt quite odd. If I were to attend, I would be attending as a reporter, as a writer looking for material, and not as someone trying to become part of that world. That world is very clearly defined and in many ways a closed one. It is closed because the lineage of the family is always there in the foreground. Theirs is a *justified* presence at these events; it has to do with land, with blood and history – the familiar history of suffering and strength. I admire all of this, but I knew I would feel my alienness even more acutely were I to attend. Maybe this was unfair to the friends, maybe a tad antisocial, but it was my way of protecting myself from the sense of being totally outside.

The truth is, I have attended a few such gatherings and my anxieties about them were not unfounded. I stay a few minutes. I am welcomed but I feel, too, that my credentials for being there are being challenged. It is not antagonistic or overt, but in the context of this rite of affirmed identity, my quest for friendship does not gel. In these family reunions in the South, expressed in the very act of gathering, I can see the blood of ownership, of home; in the rituals, in the markings on the faces – the clues of genetics – there is the meaning of family rooted in place. I may love these people and they me, but I am an outsider, an alien in this place. Our colour may be the same, but there is a strange distance. I know that my children, too, will feel this gap, this distance.

It impresses me that the meaning of America is rooted in death, family and tradition. It is. The immigrant must look elsewhere for home. Yet I knew that at some point, the myth of ownership, of being American, would confront my children. Would I have prepared them for this trauma? Will they want to be buried in South Carolina?

I am still not convinced that I want to die in America or to be buried here. Where would they plant me? Who would be my neighbours? What will the language of welcome be? Would I have to explain where I was from even in death? Would I not want to travel in the spirit realm and head for a place and a people that felt more like home? This is the kind of speculation I use to test the extent to which I feel "at home" in America. And even though now I would feel less anxious as a ghost roaming South Carolina than I would have ten years ago, I have to say that by this somewhat fanciful test, I remain psychically and emotionally an alien here. Scatter my dust in Jamaica, over a river in Castleton or in the Blue Mountains; or take it to Cape Coast to be taken up by the Atlantic waves.

CHAPTER 4

the perpetual immigrant

I call Jamaica home, but that naming is strained. There was a moment, a year or so ago, when I arrived from the UK at Charlotte International and walked through customs with the feeling of one returning "home". I argued with the officer at the baggage claim section with the righteous audacity that I have come to associate with Americans. Here I was, back "home" and somehow the airlines had lost my bag. I knew what they would say, was prepared for the promise that the bag would be on my doorstep in a day or so. I understood the language of this particular bureaucracy. I found my car and as soon as I started the engine, I felt in command. I knew the landscape, understood the flow of traffic, had no anxieties about hurtling my vehicle at over seventy miles per hour along the clotted inter-State between Charlotte and Columbia, South Carolina. In London I did not dare to drive; I rode on trains or on buses convinced that I could not negotiate the narrow roads, the strange roundabouts, the gear-shifting of manual cars, and the in-and-out of traffic, the grammar of its language – looks, nods, stares, etc. This, on the other hand, felt like home. This was where I had learned to drive, this was where I understood when to slow to within the speed limit and when I could speed slightly. I knew what to expect were I to be stopped by the police. The imminence of seeing my family after three weeks in another country made it quite clear that I was coming "home". I have done this return many times now, and every time, the sense of home has increased, become more indisputable. South Carolina is home. But I am a foreigner. That too is a fact, and while two of my children are American, and while we have lived in this country for fourteen years, and away from Jamaica for nearly twenty years, I still struggle with this notion of coming "home". I am a foreigner. My accent betrays me every time I open my mouth. I am proud of this because my struggle with the "home" question has everything to do with my relationship with America. I have always cheered for underdogs like the Cubans when they are pitted against the bullish Americans. I have in me a strong suspicion of the American presence around the world – one that is hard to shake.

Recently, a friend of mine, a Jamaican, called to let me know that he was now an American citizen. He said it without pride or joy. He was more interested in telling me how fascinated he was with those people who wept, who declared their allegiance to the American flag with tears of rejoicing in their eyes. He could only conclude that the places they had come from were so full of hopelessness and tragedy that, for them, becoming American was tantamount to being free. He had no such sentiments. He was keeping his Jamaican passport and was going to happily boast his dual citizenship. He was not buying into the American position in the world, simply taking advantage of the benefits that come from being American. Bottom-line was that he was really "dyamn" tired of the long lines waiting to get through customs at the airport. Americans walk through undisturbed and unmolested. He was looking forward to these benefits. We laughed at this. He asked me when I was going to get my citizenship. I laughed. "You don't know I am an old Marxist, man?" I joked. He pressed. I just could not see it happening. I would have to redefine myself. I would have to abandon a series of admittedly outdated ideals about what I felt was good and righteous. I would have to see myself as an opportunist, willing to discard my Third World credentials for the sweetmeats and fleshpots of Babylon. My friend pressed on me how precarious my existence might be as a non-American. My Ghanaian passport would not guarantee a rescue effort if I was stranded in a war-torn place like Burundi or Nicaragua – or Trinidad. We would be there, together, he joked, "two big notches" sipping juice and cooling in Trinidad after a great reading – when the explosion happens. And the big American helicopters would swoop down and he would wave to me and say, "Look after yourself, Kwame; the Ghanaians soon come, sure of it." It was funny, and the scenario was slightly absurd, but the point was valid. What was I defending? I was defending the right to be called a Ghanaian. Do I speak any Ghanaian languages? No. Do I have an address in Ghana? No. Do I have any prospects of returning to Ghana to live? Not at the moment. Where is my immediate family? In Jamaica and my own children and wife live in the United States. How am I described by critics and reviewers? As Jamaican. So I am defending a connection that is rooted in a sense of nationality that is self-evidently tenuous. I am more connected with Jamaica than I am with Ghana. My children will be more aware of their Jamaican connection than their Ghanaian connection. So why am I so determined to remain Ghanaian? The answer is childish, but no less real for that. I am not sure I want to be an American. I just don't think I could risk it, for my father's spirit would certainly return to haunt me and destroy all my peace. Maybe this is where the whole thing is buried: in my father's intense distrust of America. He vowed never to set foot in America and he never did. He went everywhere else, from China to the Middle East, all over Europe to the USSR. He was in Cuba, all over the Caribbean, and he was deeply connected to West Africa and to the United Kingdom. But he avoided America,

61

even in transit. He had more noble reasons: he was a Marxist, an openly avowed one at that. I am not a Marxist. I have never belonged to a political party. In Jamaica in the 1970s I was sympathetic to the People's National Party because I was attracted to its then politics of socialism – and anyway, my father was a socialist. But I cannot say that my political affiliations have driven my aversion to becoming an American.

The truth is more complicated. I struggle with the all-consuming weight of American culture. I struggle with what I will become affiliated to if I accept American citizenship. I will become affiliated to a country that has been notorious for its bullying tactics all over the world, for its endorsement of very deadly dictators and for its engagement in wars that can only be described as detrimental to the wellbeing of the societies that they claimed to be defending. I understand the place of the black person in this society and the quagmire of being a black immigrant in a country that has a remarkable history of abusing and denigrating its own black people. I cannot evade this understanding. I find solace in being an outsider when I think of the destruction of the Native Americans that characterized the formation of this country. I take comfort from the fact that I am not a direct victim of this madness, that I grew up with a sense of my own dignity and with every opportunity to assert my equality to anyone else in terms of my colour. I grew up assured of my identity and only bothered by race when I was long assured of my worth. I grew up in societies in which, as the movement deeper and deeper into post-colonial independence took place, the emerging nationalism was inextricably linked with a sense of racial pride. Ghana was deeply involved in the Pan-African movement and established strong racial ties with Black America. Marcus Garvey was part of the Ghanaian sense of self – the black star in the middle of the flag represents that famous Black Star Line fleet that Garvey had hoped would establish the beginnings of a new economic order in Africa. W.E.B. DuBois had chosen to live and die in Ghana and Ghanaians recognized that as a clear statement of racial connectedness. While race was not constructed and understood in Ghana in the ways that it was understood in the Americas, it was still a part of the imagination and sensibility of Ghanaians. We loved Muhammed Ali because he was black. We appreciated Malcolm X because he chose, as a black man, to come to Ghana. We could see around us more and more black Americans coming to live and work in Ghana. Being black was something I understood to be good when I was in Ghana. When I moved to Jamaica, I watched a movement in the '70s from the privileging of brownness and near whiteness to the celebration of blackness. Being black in Jamaica in the seventies was important. Michael Manley understood this and somehow managed to become the black candidate in his electoral campaigns against the Syrian-Jamaican, Edward Seaga, despite the fact that Manley was, for all intents and purposes, what Jamaicans would describe as white or "red". He achieved this by embracing black culture, black language, black music and speaking with utter conviction about the future of the black man – as if he was talking about himself. (He also married a black, afro-haired woman.) We believed him because he appeared to believe himself. Having grown up with that kind of affirmation and sometimes militant sense of black pride, with the expectation that our leaders would be black, it was hard to give it all up for the deeply troubling world of the American racial past and present.

America reminds me of a high school in Jamaica in my youth that was dominant in just about everything, even though it was younger than some of the old prestigious schools and lacked the tradition of "pedigree". Kingston College was the dominant school during my high school years and its success made it brashly, even amazingly, confident. I am convinced that even when its teams had less talent than its opponents, Kingston College won out of habit. I admired it even as I grew to dislike it. My school had prestige – so many national leaders were alumni and yet what I learned was the culture of losing with pride. Whenever we managed to upset this dominant school, the victory was remarkably sweet. I grew to enjoy the status of underdog and finding value in humour, irony and tradition over the brute force of unmitigated power. To give up those values (albeit ones that did not instill a dogged determination to win at all costs), for the implicit values of Kingston College through a school transfer would have been an act of betrayal, a moral failure. I would be joining a winning team, but giving up on the team that shaped me. It was a tempting prospect – the greater probability of winning – but it just seemed to be an act of defeat. In many ways, becoming an American would feel like that to me. Entirely impractical, but compellingly persuasive, this emotional sense of loyalty.

It is the challenge of bringing up children that has brought such questions into focus. Now I can no longer make the smug answer of my Nebraska debacle: "I am leaving in a few weeks, I am quite proud to say." I can't play that enjoyable game now. Now I am here because, right now, this may be the best place for us. We have contemplated and are still contemplating other options. We have thought about Jamaica, but I find that to be the least appealing option. I am not sure I could teach at the University of the West Indies, nor am I sure I could stand living with the level of violence that eats at Jamaican society. Jamaica would mean a change in our financial status, mean a whole new readjustment for the children. In any case, Jamaica has not offered me or my wife a job. These answers feel trite and deeply unpatriotic. But they are true. I would probably struggle more as a writer living in Jamaica than in the United States. So Jamaica is a difficult option. There is Canada, an attractive option, for in many ways Canada seems more manageable than the United States. But there is the complication of finding work, finding a new home and adjusting. But Canada is an option because of its proximity. Then there is the United Kingdom. It was thinking about the United Kingdom as an option that brought everything into relief for me. London is my wife's city. She was born there, grew up there, left there when she was about ten and returned after university in Jamaica. She left England to come to Canada to marry me. She has friends and relatives in London. It is her home town. She has a British passport. She has always regarded London as home, sometimes even more than Jamaica – sometimes.

And I too am connected to London. But the question of finding home is complicated by the very existence of these options. Have we become so nomadic that we are willing to go anywhere? There are theories that this has become the condition of many blacks in the New World. The gene of travel instilled in us during the Middle Passage has created a restless and adaptable people. We will go anywhere, settle anywhere, call anywhere home. But I am not really talking about the struggle to find "home" when I speak of these other possible moves, but about the pragmatics of living – the tough questions about making ends meet, or my family's security. After all, if anyone in my family were to be deported from this country, it would be me. I am the Third World child in this family. But beyond these pragmatics, the question of "home" still needles me.

I have described myself as being seen by critics and reviewers as a Jamaican writer. But since I was not born in Jamaica, defining what Jamaica means to me is always complicated. I can pretend that my Africanness and blackness were never a source of concern while I lived in Jamaica, but that would be a lie. I first learned about a peculiar brand of national and racial prejudice in Jamaica. Jamaica's history of slavery and colonialism has ensured that blackness has been associated both with Africa and, consequently, with a negative construction of self. Terms like "Guinea man" or "Congo man" were never especially endearing terms in Jamaica. As a young Ghanaian boy, I represented a trace of origin that was not always welcomed by some black or brown Jamaicans. There were those who engaged in an amnesiac ritual of treating their history and identity as something that began with Jamaica, of pretending that there was no world before Jamaica. Slavery was the beginning of Jamaica and Jamaicanness and the memory of Africa was disturbing because Africa was associated with the savage, primitive backwardness of pro-slavery propaganda. There was even, in some quarters, a strange gratitude for having been taken out of Africa – rescued, really, from the fate of the rest of Africa. Later, I would see this same thinking replicated in America. It is a profoundly disturbing, psychically bizarre, distortion of the reality of selfhood, but it was real enough when I was growing up in Jamaica. It was not a view that all held. Indeed, it was largely a middle-class view, and of those aspiring to middle-classness, who recognized the pattern of privilege and colour as being inextricably linked. So Jamaica taught me about prejudice because I was a victim of this prejudice – a prejudice of such tragic irony and such tragic comedy that it was difficult to contend with, or to cope with.

I spent much of my time during those early years in Jamaica, when I was nine, ten and eleven, battling the ignorance of Jamaicans about Africa and things African. I could tell that my mother, as a Ghanaian, was constantly given a hard time by all ranks of society about her Africanness. They asked daft questions about her comfort with clothes, about how people dressed in Africa, about cars, about the food we ate, and so on. The problems were exacerbated by the fact that my mother was my father's second wife. The first was a brilliant Jamaican theatre director who was quite well-known in the country. I have learned over the years that the marriage between my father and his first wife was regarded as a perfect match among the pseudo-elites and the artistic community in Jamaica. He was, after all, an Oxford man and she was on her way to great things as a UWI graduate who would soon head off to Yale where she would eventually get her Ph.D. as a theatre director. The news of the demise of their marriage did not sit well with these Jamaicans.

Africa, for the middle-class Jamaican imagination, evinced the same kind of response as the religious Victorians made to the Darwinian proof of relationship between humans and monkeys: they look so much like us, but don't tell me we came from them! Africans, in other words, were not exactly associated with racial pride and dignity by mentally colonized Jamaicans. This is a generalization, but a fair one. When Garvey started to advocate repatriation to Africa, he did muster a following among poor black Jamaicans, but he also secured for himself a grand opposition. Editorials in the newspaper made it clear that going back to Africa would be a backward step into the savagery from whence Jamaicans had been rescued. The system of slavery had been horrendous, but that was a long time ago, and how could we question God's wondrous wisdom in ordering human affairs. Africa had become associated with spiritual deviancy and with the obeah man, the myal man, the pocomania adherent, all people who had sustained, despite much legal oppression and censure, a sense of Africa in their communities. Then Africa became associated with Rastafarians who started to take Garvey at his word and speak very forcefully and creatively about going back to Africa.

And many did go, many, including an "uncle" of mine, Uncle Ferdy, an exceptional carpenter, who ended his African sojourn in Ghana no longer a Rastaman but a thoroughgoing rumhead. Ferdy would come to our home each Christmas and drink himself into a stupor after handing us hand-crafted gifts of toy guns and toy dolls, and the like. He would vomit in the house and sleep for long hours. That was Ferdy. When he returned to Jamaica, to Spanish Town, in the seventies to retire, he had long given up the vision of repatriation to Africa. In my childhood, Africa was Rastafarian and Rastas were the lowest of the low in middle-class eyes. My brother was given the name Unka – as in Unka, Unka, kill, kill – a simulation of the chant of cannibalistic Africans. I was labelled Little Unka or Young Unka.

Our need for survival, our desire to battle this kind of racial prejudice, helped build in us an instinct for nostalgia. It was one of many ways to cope with the insult. There were other ways, far more amusing and perhaps more satisfying. My sister and I – the one closest in age to me, Adjoa – found ourselves together at Shortwood Practising School for two years. She started in grade five and I in grade four. We exchanged stories about the insults we had undergone. At first it was difficult. Jamaican dialect or nation language is *not* English. It is a complex and difficult language to master. I thought I spoke fairly good English – in fact I had acquired a British accent after two years in London – so that, even mingled with my strong Ghanaian accent, should have ensured that I could be understood. But while I was understood by the teachers and the students, I could not understand them. They did not speak English, despite their claims to the contrary. For the first six months I struggled, trying my best to follow the dance and turn of the Jamaican language. At that age, Jamaican children did not (and I'm sure still do not) have the subtlety of bilingualism – they simply shouted louder when I said, "Eh?" The teacher felt pity and started to translate for me in class. But her St. Catherine accent was rather thick and this added to a comedy of errors and confusion. But I did well in class. I could read and that helped. Yet, my difference posed problems because the other children decided to try out their knowledge of Africa. This was gleaned from such authoritative sources as Tarzan movies, Hollywood films like *The African Queen*, Phantom comics, and the very reliable knowledge of older brothers and sisters. So I was tested: "Did I like shoes? Did I live in a house? Did I know Tarzan? Did I ever see a tiger, an elephant, a cheetah, a lion, a chimpanzee…? Did I like to wear clothes? Did I see women's

titties out a door, all the time? Did I ever meet the Phantom?"
At first I was defensive and embarked on a futile education
campaign. It was not what they wanted to hear. If I denied
anything, they would call me a liar. So I lied. I lied first about
eating snakes. They enjoyed that and I decided to embellish.
I developed such an uncanny system of lying about things that
it was soon common knowledge that I had met Tarzan and
that I did not like him because he still talked like an ape and
contrary to the impression given by the comics, he did not
wear a loincloth, but went around *grossly* naked. My stories
grew in grandeur, possessed of the spirit of seventeenth century
explorers like Walter Raleigh or tale-weavers like Hakluyt. The
other children devoured the stories. So I kept feeding them
these tales.

When, after a few months, there began to be a dawning sense
of distrust, (it may have been when I started to talk about the
pet lion I had at home), I came up with an ingenious strategy
for deflecting their suspicions. From then on, when I was
challenged about anything, I would tell them to go ask my sister.
She agreed to everything. And when I was approached by her
older, but equally gullible friends, I would answer with such
flippant boredom and hint of impatience, while embellishing
for more effect, that they bought it all. I still say to myself: Ah,
the fools. For they *were* fools to believe all of this, but they could
not be entirely blamed for their ignorance. Our action was one
of self-protection, of self-preservation, for we were being insulted
all the time and it was difficult, very difficult. But we took secret
pleasure in our game.

It was within the context, then, of some personal hostility
and strongly negative feelings towards Africa, that we developed
our nostalgia for Ghana. Ghana was a place of great stories,
family stories. We preserved stories like most families do, by
passing on tales of the exploits of one child to the rest of the
children. There were five of us, and between us we had enough

stories to go around and around until they formed the fabric of nostalgia.

There was the story of my older brother who brought a stone, almost twice his size, instead of a switch when my mother asked him to bring something for her to beat him with. He was two and understood irony.

There was the story of that same brother who drove the car at age four, down a hill and into a ditch – he lived to tell the tale, as he did when he was ten and set the entire field of corn and grass at the back of our house afire. He was punished by having to walk out with a bucket, stark naked, to try and battle the blaze.

The story of our first communal whipping for missing school, the story of my infant brother who drained all the glasses of liquor left by guests after one of my father's parties, and became so drunk that he assumed the position of a Chief: "Bring me my chokota!!" We would repeat the story and roll with laughter – and the story of my accidents, the poisonous plants I ate, the pills I consumed, the car that ran over me and left me for dead, and so on.

There were songs too, songs of our childhood in Ghana, songs that reminded us of our grandparents, our grandmother singing her Gospel songs in Fanti on the last day we would see her while she waited for the car to come around and take her to the bus station, to take her back to Cape Coast. We would sing the song with sadness and my mother would weep. We remembered the house, the school, the university campus, the fresh bread we would gut on our way back from the bakery located at the top of the hill in Legon, the games we played at the Africa Centre, trying to mimic the professional dancers and drummers of the theatre company there.

We recited these tales of remembrance as people trying to ensure that the memory of our origins was not lost. It was part of who we were and we had no good reason to battle that nostalgia for it sustained us. So the names of our relatives, our cousins, our friends had the sound of a litany – a strange cadence that remained locked in the mind like a song. Nostalgia was rich: the fufu, the banku, the kenke, the kelewele, the okra soup, the palm nut soup, the groundnut soup, the yoyi tree, the akra, the garri done a million ways, the monumental legend of the day Aba, my older sister, and I ate plates and plates of boiled yam and stewed corned beef with that thin film of softness over the mildly flavoured tuber, until we were almost sick, but how we relished that meal and how we remembered it as a legend of incredible proportions.

We could afford the nostalgia of Ghana because Ghana was a place of childhood and the complications of coups, of political intrigue, of the corruption of the Government, of the executions and the arrests – while a part of our imagination and quite acutely remembered – remained muted by the relative safety that we felt as children, protected by the fear of our parents. It was their task to fear. We had to leave Accra in a hurry to speed to Cape Coast and remain there for nearly a week in the middle of a school term. It did not occur to us that my father was actually running for his life and trying to avoid deportation for his political actions. We did not know. All I remember of that trip was the excitement of a sudden departure and my father getting sick on whiskey and coconut water – apparently a horrendous combination. It was the first time that I had seen him become sick like Uncle Ferdy. There was a sense of foreboding and sadness about that time, but it passed and we were soon happily running around playing games with our cousins.

I would learn later that my father was actually ordered to be deported, but that the order was rescinded because someone had spoken to Nkrumah on his behalf. I found this out when I saw a clipping from the *Gleaner* in Jamaica that indicated that he had actually been deported: "University Professor deported."

71

He was never deported, but that was part of the excitement of those times, and we could transform even this moment of potential catastrophe into a nostalgic memory.

And there were more memories of gunfire at night during coups, the news of Kotoka's dramatic and tragic killing, the flight of Nkrumah after the coup that ousted him, and so on. I even sang songs about the Biafran war – but we were children, and it is part of the condition of children to be able to alchemize the hardships of life into a litany of nostalgia and adventurous memory.

So in Jamaica we held onto Ghana as a place of hope. We wanted to return, and we felt with our mother when she walked through the house singing Ghanaian songs in Fanti and Ewe, singing songs that invoked her mother. We mourned with her when her father was dying and she was not able to go and see him. We mourned, too, when her mother died and she had to go home to be there with the family. And even as time began to erode our connection with Ghana, we preserved the memory always. It was our way of sustaining ourselves and finding dignity in our Africanness. I embraced my Africanness gladly.

By the time I was eleven, I had abandoned calling myself Neville and started to call myself Kwame. I was linked up nicely with the Rastafarians who liked to talk to me, liked to connect with someone from the Motherland.

CHAPTER 5

in transit: secret selves

All the time we lived in Jamaica, I had the sense that I would be leaving to go somewhere else. The year and a half spent "in transit" in London in 1971 fixed that feeling in all of us. It was a year and a half of being unsettled, rootless. During that time we learned to be always ready to move. I never understood how defining that period was until recently. It was a year or so of dreams. Our days were spent in speculation about our future. It was a rough and yet an important time for the family.

Mostly, I remember that we lived like campers, nomads. We were poor. We had become, quite suddenly and unexpectedly, poor. The problem was that my father was caught between jobs. The decision to leave Ghana had not been sudden, but the execution of the move was clearly not brilliantly planned. The idea, as far as I can determine, was for my mother to travel to England with us, the children, and wait a few weeks for my father to tie up ends in Ghana. He would join us briefly in London and then go ahead to Jamaica to prepare a place for us. We would follow shortly after. The job in Jamaica was a government appointment at the Institute of Jamaica. At that time the Jamaican Labour Party was in power under Hugh Shearer, a brown-skinned Jamaican, a longtime trade unionist.

Edward Seaga, who would take over the party not long after this, was actually the one who appointed my father to the post. It all seemed quite progressive: the first black man in such a position and all that.

My father was giving up his intense love of teaching to assume an administrative position. He accepted the offer because of his patriotism, his desire to give something back to Jamaica, and to give some time to his ageing mother. In letters to his friends in Jamaica, it is clear that my father had wanted to return to Jamaica even before he was offered the job. In fact, most of the letters of that period were concerned with his efforts to get an appointment at the University of the West Indies, at Mona. These efforts fell through – the result, he felt, of someone's pettiness. At one stage an appointment in Barbados was talked of, but he either rejected it, or it too fell through. I am not sure how the Institute appointment came about, but it was evidently not completely settled before he resigned his lectureship in Ghana. Had it been settled, our "in transit" stop in London would not have become the extended limbo that it was.

My father may have decided to leave Ghana because he had become disillusioned with Nkrumah's great socialist project, which had collapsed to a coup d'etat. On the evidence of letters to friends, my father's optimism about Ghana's political future had faltered. He seemed more cynical, less idealistic and fired-up than he had been in the early sixties. We did not know any of this, and if we had, we probably would not have understood it. What we did know was that we were embarked on a great migration. It would change things for ever.

The three or four weeks in London became almost two years. My father got caught in a dispute with the University of Ghana about the home in which we had lived in Legon. Without my mother there to argue, to challenge and to question, my father ended up giving up a great deal of money to satisfy the whims of the University's clerks. Now more broke than expected and still smarting at the amount of money on his booze tabs at the various clubs at the University, my father finally moved to London after we had been there for several months.

They had been hard months of moving from room to room – from Earls Court to other places in the city. Five children and a mother. We were a big family and feeding us, dressing us, being with us was difficult. My mother stretched the savings, but soon her letters to Neville asking him to send money went unheeded. It was clear that she would have to find some work or some source of income. She went for both. She worked in the kitchen at the Cumberland Hotel in the West End and did some off-track betting to augment her savings. She was doing grunge work: this artist, this university-educated woman of dignity and pragmatic humility. She worked. She worked. She would come home tired, feet in pain. We could tell that she was working hard.

Nothing was permanent. We lived out of suitcases. All our books, toys, household items, furniture – all the objects that had made our house in Ghana a home – had been crated and shipped to Jamaica. We would lose most of that stuff to Customs in Jamaica who made it almost impossible for us to pay the duty on those things by quoting ludicrous prices. Even the suitcases and boxes of shoes and clothing we had bought in London they seized. Duty was demanded. The money was not there, and the goods stayed for a few months in Customs and then disappeared. I lost my first pair of Clarks with that important patent leather look and the carefully crafted designs, all pimples and dots. The tough leather soles were preserved by a few rows of these metal strips called Blakeys – I had been desperate for shoes like this, which were all the rage in London. We lost them. For years, I would remember my Clarks with deep sadness and resentment at the Customs people. I imagined some son of a Customs officer profiling in my good shoes. There were no good Clarks in Jamaica. Nor were there the olive-green flannel suits, one of which I had lost as well. It was in the suitcase along with most of the good clothes my mother had managed to purchase during a grand shopping expedition before we finally left London for Jamaica.

In that year and a half in London, clothes became important to me. It was during that time that I began to have an inward sense of my personality. In Ghana, the only hints at a personality amounted to anecdotes about me doing things that I am not certain I recall myself. For the most part, these "defining" recollections were part of our family lore. My self-awareness was as yet undefined. Childhood in Ghana was stable, though not void of trauma. There was the death of Arabna, a playmate who lived a few houses away in the sprawling housing complex of modern white-brick two-storey homes.

When Arabna died, a wail carried into our home: "Arabna weh woo!" It was a woman's lamentation: long, wrenching, and haunting. It would not stop. Arabna was six years old and she had choked on fufu. It was impossible to believe that our friend was gone. The mourning went on for days and the house she lived in became, for us, a gloomy hole, a place of lost childhood. It was a trauma, but hardly a defining one, except in one important sense: it presented me with the fickleness of life and the almost comic simplicity of accidental death. I knew then that a lump of fufu should not kill anyone. We all ate fufu. For quite some while afterwards our parents kept telling us to not talk while we ate. This is all it would have taken and Arabna would have lived. We stopped talking with food in our mouths. But for me it was painfully comic. The same sensation would come over me when my mother and I waited, sixteen years later, for the phone call announcing the passing of my father. Comic. Absurd. Painful.

Even the fact that, as a child in Ghana, accidental death seemed fated to be my undoing appears to have marked me only physically. The collecting and repetition of these tales of close calls had the effect of ritualizing and thus almost fictionalizing the moment. It helped us to manage the pain, if there was pain. I have come to see this family practice, which affirmed the individual quirks and narratives of each member, as perhaps the most stabilizing force in our lives. My parents understood the power of storytelling and myth-making and they passed it on to us. What I remember of my car accident is largely a blur. But the details were added in each retelling.

I hold on to the accident because it forces me to think of Ghana most days of my life. I was seven and had somehow been left by my siblings to find my way home from school. There were two significant obstacles in the journey. The first was to cross the main road, which was not a busy thoroughfare but was busy enough for a seven year old. The second was the stretch of bushes that separated each housing complex from the next. These bushes had footpaths, but the dense stretches of vegetation were infested with snakes – serious snakes. The only way to make it through the bushes alone, as far as I knew, was to sprint the entire way until you came to the opening on the far side of our backyard.

Sprinting blindly was not, however, the solution for the main road. I ran. I did not see the car coming but I saw it going – a sky-blue sedan – and that puzzled me while I lay quite shocked on the asphalt. I was waiting for it to stop. I had not experienced the business of car accidents, but I knew that the fact that the car was still moving was an absurdity. I stared at the tail smoke, then the brilliant sky. I could not move. I did not feel able to move. Time collapsed after that. I can't tell how long I lay there or when the white shirt of a teacher came into view. They knew me, the hands that lifted me from the road. I saw the white Volkswagen bug they were taking me to, remember the red upholstery and the way the front seat folded forward to fit me into the back. I remember, then, being embarrassed at the bloody mess I was making. My shirt was completely red and the people holding me seemed to be bleeding as well. They say I was quite lucid. I talked a lot. At the hospital I remember the gravel of the driveway and then I blacked out. I was in an examination room with people around when I came to. What I heard the doctor (one Dr. Frinpong) say was reassuring. He said there was no real brain damage from the vicious blow I took on the head, from where blood sprouted and crimsoned everything. Afterwards he said I had held tightly to a clutch of movie-star chewing-gum cards and that, as long as I was conscious, I was explaining each cowboy to those who were around. I would not let them go. Frinpong said this meant I was not going to suffer brain trauma.

I blame him, though, for the mangling of my right ankle. It had been crushed by the wheels of the car. The foot was placed in a cast that I wore for weeks. It became a nuisance when, as was his custom, my father punished me by sending me into a corner to kneel down. I could not kneel because the cast ended above my knee. I have always assumed that I had broken only my ankle, but some other fracture must have occurred. When the cast was removed, my foot was deformed. I had no jutting anklebone on the inside of my right foot but the outside bones jutted out obscenely. My foot was turned slightly inwards. Frinpong assured my mother that I would "grow out of it".

I have not. I suffer pains because of this ankle. I live with this pain. According to recent x-rays, the bones are loose in the ankle. They slip in and out of the wrong grooves. I have to find the best position, the best pressure spot to work things into place. Sometimes I simply limp gingerly on it, stiffly, afraid of the sudden consuming pinch on a nerve.

I remember Ghana. I remember that I was surrounded by black leaders, black teachers, black doctors, black writers – I had taken it all for granted. Nationalism was easy because race was hardly an issue.

Ironically, I grew up with a strange complex that made me associate whiteness with a negative sense of self. In Ghana I was teased for being white. I was called "obroni". This was more defining. It was not about life and death, but it was about the way I would begin to shape my own understanding of race. I have not, in any other society, been called white or anything close to it. My complexion is hard to describe, but photographs would assure anyone that whatever whiteness was in our family genes (as I mentioned earlier, my Jamaican great-grandparents were the products of a mixture of slaves and white Irish immigrants to Jamaica), little appeared in me. But *I* was "obroni". Not my siblings, who were all darker than I was. It may have had to do with the fact that my father was a lighter-hued black man from abroad. For obroni did not simply mean white man, it also meant foreigner, alien.

My nose was the other culprit. Obviously African in its spread and substance, it tended to announce itself too loudly for comfort's sake because I was always blowing it, pulling at it, sneezing from it, and picking at it because of my chronic sinus problem (another diagnosed as "he will grow out of it" – this by Frinpong and a British doctor in London – both were wrong) and the allergy I had to cigarette smoke. My parents smoked chronically. My nose was constantly inflamed and I was nicknamed "cherry-blossom nose". Not an original idea, but one that bothered me. Combined with "obroni", I was taking the worst disenfranchisement. There was no language available to me to articulate pride in being in any measure close to whiteness. I would have to learn that re-actionary and self-hating language in England, Jamaica and, most eloquently, in America. In Ghana, I made up for the absence of such a language with absurdity. The conversation I had with my amused mother on these issues is one that she repeats as evidence of my ability as a freethinking artist.

"I am not obroni! I am not white!"

"Who said you are obroni?"

"Everybody. I am not obroni. I am not white!"

"No? Oh, so what are you then?"

"I am... I am... I am green!"

We did not have a television set at the time and Kermit's song had not yet been written, so this was a wholly original thought that made my mother fall about laughing and retelling the tale to anyone she saw. I was pleased with my ability to finally settle the issue of my colour.

For the poet looking around for childhood germs of the future, my answer is clear genius. The truth is more prosaic; I had few options when my mother asked what I was. I could have said black, but I knew it was not entirely true, but I also knew something deeper: that my greatest objection to the name "obroni" was that it made me alien with a particular and negative identity. It made me a known antagonist, a known stranger. It placed me squarely in the limited Ghanaian dialect of race and left me with little that was useful. It was not that I minded being different. In fact, I liked being different, but *I* wanted to define that difference.

Perhaps I had no real understanding of colour at the time; perhaps green was a colour I blurted out because of the pressure to say something, anything. But I don't think so. I think I turned to green because I had understood something about race and racism, something about self-awareness and identity. It would characterize the rest of my life. Being green was not about denying my blackness, or whiteness, for that matter. Sitting here more than thirty years later, and retrieving this as myth, offers a wonderful opportunity for fanciful interpretation. I now treat that moment, which I recall only as a memory granted me by my mother and siblings, as sweetly symbolic. The details of the language clearly belong to my mother and her telling, but not the emotions, which I recall quite well and associate very specifically with Cape Coast where we spent summers with my Pentecostal grandmother and our wild and engaging cousins (the ones who first called me *obroni*), with the smell of yeast and baking bread that my grandmother made in an outdoor mud kiln and sold for a living, with the rugged Atlantic coast, with missing my parents. I regard these memories as important groundings for much that I write. The way I retrieve them and grant them a certain symbolic quality is symptomatic of my inclinations as a poet so that, in many ways, these memories are the seeds of my poetry writing, and the earliest signs of the shaping of a personality, the original DNA traces of the clown, mimic and artist that I would become.

These anecdotal hints of a personality would join other stories to form a received sense of self. But before I developed a secret life, my sense of being an individual, of having a private self, was undefined. For example, my sense of being a good child who would do anything to reduce tension and conflict in the house, was, like many things that come to define who we think we are, a product of another series of stories handed to me. The closeness I felt for my older sister Aba was rooted in the family myth of the famous shared meal. What I remember most about that incident was that, after a while, I continued to eat more and more, not so much because I was relishing the food, but because I could sense a love and solidarity emerging between my sister and I.

There were other stories for the archives. There was the day we all cut school to go and play with a white boy who had a house full of toys. All four of us went roaming through Legon looking for mischief. We settled on visiting this white boy whose parents must have been some kind of American diplomats in Ghana. Maybe they were British, but the story works better if they were American. This visit confirmed what we had always suspected: that white people had a lot more fun in life than we did. He did not seem to go to school and he had all kinds of toys. We did not care too much for him – he was a spoilt brat – but we scavenged his toys, playing with them and enjoying them. For us, America was toy heaven.

This was not the only evidence of American superabundance. There was, apparently, a good trade in second-hand furniture, kitchen utensils, and other household items owned usually by American and sometimes European (rarely English) diplomats or expatriates who would leave the country suddenly for a variety of reasons: coups, diplomatic fracas, anxiety about encroaching Marxism, and so on. My mother, always the entrepreneur, was constantly in search of good deals. We would accompany her to these places and burden the car with games: Monopoly, Stratego, Scrabble – and with toys, utensils, anything that did not seem completely overused. The revelation, of course, was the material plenty of these people. White people, we could tell, defined their lives by material things. The objects were well-preserved. We, on the other hand, found these toys to be quite disposable – as disposable as the cardboard dolls we would make ourselves, dressing them in the silver and gold wrappers from cigarette cartons – designer fashions of some genius. For these dolls, we built houses, cars, submarines, aeroplanes – all from boxes and scraps. Manufactured toys would come in waves, but these, our homemade toys, were our mainstay. We were good at entertaining ourselves.

But the day we cut school to indulge in Americana, we also faced a serious and unprecedented round of whippings. My mother actually had to borrow a cane from a neighbour to exact our punishment. She had discovered we were missing by chance. One of us had forgotten his or her lunch. When my mother arrived at the school, she learnt that we were not there. She panicked. We had been kidnapped – all of us. She called the police, called relatives, called friends. The prospect of losing us in one fell swoop was unbearable.

In the meantime, I had grown tired of America. I wanted to return to the comforts of the Third World. I was whining and complaining, arguing that what we were doing was wrong. Our leader, my eldest brother, Kojo, tried to cow me into silence. It did not work. Eventually, they made the mistake of sending me away. "Crybaby!" he teased. My sisters did not come to my defence. So I ran through the bushes, frightened to death and terribly uncertain. When I came to the edge of our backyard, I saw my mother. She grabbed me, held me close. I started to cry.

"Where are the others?"

I pointed.

"Where, where?"

I explained. She sent me inside. My brother hated me. He got the worst of the punishment, at least if one went by the howling he made. I got the least: the value of copping a plea bargain as a snitch, I suppose. My eldest sister, actually, may have been the most severely tested because she chose to be defiant and not cry. My brother, skilled and experienced in being punished with beatings, knew that early, melodramatic caterwauling reduced the punishment. Stoic, tearless silence simply annoyed the punisher. Aba cried eventually, but by then she had received more than any of us weaker souls.

Excursions to America were clearly not a good thing. This idea, too, would last. For me, the label of a good boy was taking shape. I was the good one. It would take London and the development of a secret life to complicate my personality, to provide me with a layered sense of myself.

Retrieving such instances of personality-shaping, particularly those connected with Ghana, is, in fact, a process of recovering the path of a writer and artist, just as being the son of my father helps to define much of what I have become and may give clues as to what I will become as my years of fatherhood continue.

Ghana, my life there, and the manner of my encounter with America in that country, still affects what I feel about America today. Dreamer that my father was, he provided an ideological framework for me that was constantly crashing against stark reality. It has always been the shock of the clash between dream and reality that has sustained me or moved me as a writer, as a person fascinated by people. The London my father painted for us – the London we had seen briefly on visits to Oxford where we lived out his dream of British rural quiet – came heavily up against the poverty and struggle of the London we had to survive for two years in the early seventies. Jamaica, too, was a shadow offered by my father, and by the time I hit America, I was prepared for revelations. They came, too.

I write about the hardships in London now because in many ways it was in London that I first began to understand race and the self. It was my constant anxiety that the world I was offering my children during their formative years was so different and antithetical to the world I experienced as a child. I worried, in other words, that they were being tossed into the quagmire of racial bipolarity before ever experiencing the alternative world of being black in a black country. My worry may be unfounded since my wife survived quite fine, despite being born in London and living there until she was eleven. It is no doubt impossible to know what ultimately defines who we are, and whether our attitudes to race and self can really be shaped by altering the environment in which we live. But it must mean something significant to grow up in a world where all the models of social success, authority, intellect, and creativity are black. It must suggest possibility, your capacity to do these things. Not just the capacity, but almost the inevitability of being in these positions. In Ghana, there was no debate about where the black engineers were, or the black doctors, or architects or classical musicians; they were there in Ghana. By the end of the colonial period, there was no one else to do those jobs. Possibility.

I learned the fine art of willing dreams into being because of Barbara Chisholm. She was a secret I kept for a long time. Eventually – I could not help myself – I blurted it out that I liked Barbara Chisholm. By then she was a regular in my dreams. We were living in a worn, damp flat on Bormer Road – 14 Bormer Road – which was owned by an old Haitian man called Mr. Hercules. I am not even certain of the spelling of the street name any more. About ten years after we had lived there, we went back to try and find the street, the house. Neither existed. There were monolithic high-rises where the old houses had been and the entire terrain was different. There was nothing familiar. This may have been what Hercules was holding out against, but I don't think his motives were so noble. But his name suited him: Mr. Hercules. He lived with his son, Felix, and his two daughters, Hannah and Sabrina, upstairs above the rooms we rented with their linoleum-covered floors and the worn olive/curry coloured carpet, pocked with dark brown holes and stains that made the carpet seem wet all the time. The rooms smelt of leaking gas and the residual odour of cooking locked into the house, along with all the precious warmth that we could keep inside. Hercules had managed to hold up the demolition of the houses he owned in this area, that were to be replaced by council flats. We watched as house after house was demolished to rubble. The pub across the road from our place was the last to go. After that, it would be us. Mr. Hercules would not sell. He was waiting for a good deal.

He was a short, slight, dark man with prominent veins in his forehead. He always dressed in grey, smartly attired most of the time. He had a leather briefcase. I did not know where he worked or if he worked at all. But he was always busy going in and out of the house while the neighbourhood systematically crumbled to rubble.

Perhaps he had taken us in because it would help his cause, though no doubt he also needed the rent money. But it was clear that we made a perfect picture for his campaign: a poor family of five children and a hard-working woman looking after them alone, because her husband was away. (My father had left after only a few weeks at Bormer Road to go to Jamaica.) How could anyone throw them out? How? The officials would visit – men in white suits clambering up the mangy carpet on the stairs to disappear for an hour with Mr. Hercules. They never returned triumphant. Mr. Hercules always smiled when they had gone.

We all slept on a foldout sofa that was permanently transformed into a bed. In the beginning this was exciting. But soon we were fighting for space to stretch or just to live. Bormer Road was good at first because it saw the bright moment when we were reunited with our sisters. For almost four months, they had been living with some distant cousins in a lovely home in London. We would see them rarely. It was such a painful time for us all. My mother was especially torn by it; one could see that she saw it as a failure. It became more and more difficult for her when the relatives trying to "bring up" the girls began to question things my mother did. It was difficult for us because we had never been split up before. It was 14 Bormer Road that brought us together. My mother asked Aba what she thought about leaving the relative comfort of our cousins' place to stay in the rundown house in Ladbroke Grove.

"As long as we are together, we will live anywhere."

Sentimental, but it came from a twelve year old. It meant everything. We would go to school together, experience our laughter and games together. It was wonderful.

By the time I began to dream of Barbara Chisholm, my mother had bought a set of deck chairs which were transformed into beds for those who could not stand sharing. The bed was emptier. I dreamt of Barbara Chisholm – her golden curly hair, her... her... actually, all I can recall is her hair. She was white. I loved a white girl. Perhaps there were no black girls to love in my class, perhaps. She looked like a character in one of the Enid Blyton books I read. She fitted my fantasy of love, a fantasy that did not include an image of myself beside her. She figured in my fictional pillars of life: the worlds of adventure, schoolboy deeds, and romance. In these worlds, my own face, my blackness, my awkwardness, my distinct Ghanaianness did not belong. I felt about Barbara the same kind of detachment that I felt when reading the literature that engrossed my attention at the time.

The Famous Five, The Five Find-Outers and Dog, Jennings, and the Billy Bunter comics were all-important in defining my sense of England. These narratives are not known for their multicultural representation. So how does a boy identify with characters who look nothing like him, whose place in the world is far removed from his? He does so through a kind of sublimation of sensibilities, an imaginative detachment. This detachment meant suppressing oneself, removing one's identity from the dialogue. I enjoyed vicariously the adventures of these children and I even imagined forming my own gang and embarking on our own adventures. It was something we would eventually attempt in Jamaica, some years later. The Seven Black Bottles gang (our symbol was a shelf of seven Red Stripe beer bottles painted with some water-based black paint) was doomed to fail, like so many ideas so thoroughly founded on a culturally alien world-view. As children, we saw this again and again.

My brother and I became increasingly fascinated by comic book superheroes. In fact, fantasies were one of the things that sustained us during those especially tough times when we were a family divided, prior to Bormer Road. My sisters were with our cousins and we boys were with our parents living in the basement of a middle-class cottage in Hounslow. It was an oppressive time for us. My father, embarrassed that the Barbadians who had rented the place to us saw us as rather pathetic, homeless types, was determined not to grant our landlords any reason to complain about our presence there. The man was probably a friend, or at least an acquaintance from Oxford. What was clear was that Neville wanted as little contact with these people as possible. He was resting because of hard times. He imposed one of the most repressive silence laws I would ever know. We had to whisper all the time – soft whispers – while we tiptoed through the home. It was as if he wanted us to disappear, to become completely invisible. I was eight years old and my brother was thirteen. We were active boys, full of energy and laughter, but for the two months in that house, we whispered. We learned to giggle silently, the pressure of our constraint hurting our ears. If we slipped and made too loud a sound, we were punished.

It must have been horrendous for my parents to have to live in this manner. My father would vanish into his basement world and count the days before things were worked out in Jamaica so we could go. My mother was increasingly angry at my father's passivity and by his draconian measures. One day we were walking outside and my mother noticed that my brother and I were still whispering and giggling in that tight, silent way. She cried even as she told us to speak up. We were not sure why. It was changing us into boys who spent most of our time imagining, trying to concoct silent distractions for ourselves.

The superheroes became the distracting obsession. We would be superheroes. It was quite clearly a fantasy of escape. We began to plot our careers and we were not constructing a fantasy world. For us it was a world of reality, a pragmatic world. We planned to build all the vehicles for our heroes and design and make the costumes. We began to make a list of all the tools and equipment we would need to build the vehicles. We identified sources and drew blueprints for the construction. We would not use engined vehicles – they would coast along, though they would only be useful for downhill conditions. The costumes were to be made out of garbage bags. We started a slow, secretive campaign to collect one bag a day. Eventually, we would have enough to make the costumes.

It did not work. The bags were impossible to cut and sew, and no one would give us the hardware for our vehicle. Our desire for escape from the tyranny of silence had turned into an elaborate, absurdist fantasy, and one based on white myths and white materialism. Spandex suits would have done perfectly well for us, but we could never afford them. We had to use garbage bags.

This attempt to suspend the self so that we could function in our imaginative world is no doubt what happened in my relationship with Barbara Chisholm. The truth is that she may not have actually registered my existence. No doubt, we saw each other in profoundly different ways. I saw her as a truth, as a figure in my narrative imagination, as an enactment, a realization of myth. Being white, she was lovable, the perfect object of my romantic ideals. But for her, I must have been an aberration. She could not have located me in *her* sense of myth or romance. So while I loved her, she could not be expected to love me in the same way. I don't know if she imagined me beyond the school. We did talk; we even walked together from school one day. I cherished these moments. But she drifted from me. Eventually she became a secret fantasy, a figure of shame the older I got. By loving her I began to see myself as odd and as a stranger. I began to carry the secret of my difference.

At school, I learned how to be quiet, how to hold in all I knew and only offer what was needed. I learned how not to embarrass myself or my family. I understood the difference; kept my home world a secret. I learned to be ashamed of the dilapidated state of our house, the poverty we dealt with. Secrets: I was growing up. I learned to keep it secret that my mother worked at the Cumberland and brought home meals for us to eat. I learned to conceal the ties – one of my father's Oxford ties – that were used to secure my trousers, which were constantly falling off my extremely skinny body. My shirt covered the secret. To reveal these secrets would be to reveal myself. I had secrets now and in this way I understood that I was growing up. More importantly, I was discovering a sense of self. It was clear that I would need this to survive in London. The secure world of Ghana was gone and had been replaced by the complications of race.

I think I became aware of being black in London. I say this tentatively because in Ghana I saw enough to recognize that colour was an issue in life. There was all that business of being called an obroni, but there was more.

There were two white men who drove in a black car onto our gravel driveway one morning. They wore dark suits and carried suitcases. It was one of those Legon mornings when the sun blazed so relentlessly it turned all the white things – the main road, the prickly cement walls and roofs of the homes, the whitewashed gutter, the sheets on the line, the concrete-tiled verandah, everything – into a painful glare that hurt the eyes. The sky was so transparent it seemed shocked white. The white shirts of the two men, who looked like Mormon evangelists, shimmered in the haze. We had gathered at the top of the stairs to listen. We had family friends who were white, but these men seemed different: they were young, clean-cut, and uncertain.

The visit lasted no longer than a few minutes. The loud boom of my father's voice began the commotion. He was ordering them out of his house even as he questioned them about who they thought he was. He was aggressive, and the quality of his anger at these two white men startled us, firstly because they were white and secondly because he rarely, when sober, became so animated either in anger or joy. The men left quickly, their necks aflame with embarrassment. My father stood at the doorway and watched them pull out of the driveway and up the hill. He then turned around, glanced quickly at us, smiling, and then muttered, "Damn CIA agents!" Then he was sitting in the living room on the phone.

We did not understand the implications of this at the time.

In fact, this story, as I have told it, may not be entirely reliable. Like most of my memories of Ghana, it combines the myth-making of collected and transmitted family lore, and the almost hero-worshipping hyperbole of stories about our parents. My mother, for example, was tagged "Mama the Great" by my father, who encouraged myth-making and hyperbole. It would have been my father who called the two men CIA agents. We accepted this. But there is little reason, even today, to doubt the credibility of this claim. The CIA was quite active in Ghana at the time, and my father was well-known by the politicians, including Kwame Nkrumah. Indeed one of the legends of our family involves a visit to Owusu Castle by my mother and my eldest brother to visit the President. That the CIA would want to use Neville as a pawn was absurd only to those who knew his politics. CIA intelligence must have been quite weak at the time to have missed that piece of information.

Yet Neville's action at that time spoke volumes to us about race. His fearlessness meant that there was no inherent authority located in the white man. We were learning this early and it would define our understanding of race in London. But it did not prepare us for much of what we would experience there. The blatant insults were almost daily and so were the fights and the need to form cliques to protect ourselves.

London, then, became a holding place, a long period of limbo that locked the idea of being in a constant state of elsewhere firmly into our minds. It did not take long for me to start seeing Jamaica not only as a place far away from Ghana, but as a place we would almost certainly leave. Yet Jamaica became home.

The beginnings of my coming to understand myself as a distinct person with secrets in his life, was the product, perhaps, of maturity, but more probably of circumstances far more complicated than what I had known in Ghana. Barbara Chisholm was my secret, though my fascination with her did not blossom into a perpetual fascination with white women. Whether this

91

would have happened had we stayed in England, I do not know. But quite soon after our arrival in Jamaica I began to add to my list of imagined girlfriends. These were the girls I liked who did not know I liked them, who had become part of my imaginative life: Andrea Watson, Barbara Coombes, Linda Wilson – names, lots of names, that come back to me now, not as whole people with personalities, but in the way that song lyrics come back to me, evoking something specific in my life.

Jamaica was nothing like I had imagined it. It was not the rural world of my father's stories, but an urban space: rough, harsh, exciting, complicated and totally foreign. I had to learn how to be Jamaican, and this, in a sense, taught me how to be Ghanaian.

'this poor pathless harbourless spade'

Part of the process of establishing myself here in America has to do with trying to define who I am in this society. I am, like everyone else, defined by what I claim about my nationality and by what I do. What I do here is teach. I am a university professor. But being a writer is more important to my inner sense of self than being a professor. (The other things I do tend to have some tangential connection to both teaching and writing. I run arts programs, work with writers, serve in the community, go to church.) The reactions of others to my writing goes a long way in shaping my moods, my attitudes to the world and the people whom I choose to surround me. For me, writing is intimate, drawing on and sometimes exposing a painfully constructed picture of the self. It is, in part, a process of expression, but I also have to acknowledge that my writing's reception is really crucial to my sense of wellbeing. I hate my work to be rejected, because such a judgement appears to be saying something about me. For many years I was often preoccupied with what it meant to say that I was a writer in America when I had not published here (not until *Midland*, published in 2003). Should this have been a problem, an issue? Perhaps not, but in many ways, I kept myself protected from despondency by cherishing the notion that there was a world outside the one I was living in that regarded what I wrote, and what I thought as relevant and of some import. I didn't have that sense in America and that played a major role in whether I felt as if I belonged or not.

So I am a writer with a peculiar dilemma that has to do with geography and the subject matter that I deal with. Even as this book unfolds, I am constantly testing the tone and quality of my own response to the business of living in America. I am led to vent, to express with no shortage of irritation and frustration, the challenges of being a writer who lives in America, writes about the Caribbean and whose work is published in the United Kingdom and Canada. The venting is tempting and quite natural because frustration is the constant condition of writers, especially poets, who have days when they are convinced that what they are writing is, quite simply, brilliant, and the work that they see being showcased in all kinds of important places is, quite simply, crap. I am all too aware that the 'manly' vigour of venting can so easily decline into whining, pathetic self-indulgence. This can feel good for a moment, but after a few days it begins to stink; there is much regret afterwards. The other instinct is to try to achieve a stoic distance, a fatalistic resignation with regard to the difficulties and, one nonchalantly assumes, the occasional rewards, of being a writer in my position. I am attracted to this option because it would make me appear a very noble and sensible individual. But it sounds far too pretentious, far too contrived.

I found some comfort in V.S. Naipaul's essay "London", published in 1958 in the *TLS* and reprinted in *The Overcrowded Barracoon*. I like Naipaul's essay because he whines a bit, but he is also quite dispassionate, and wonderfully fatalistic in that dramatic ending when he suggests that it may be that he will have to find another job, other than writing, given his situation. Of course, reading that essay almost fifty years after it was written, one's reading is biased by the fact that we know that Naipaul

94

did "make it", that he has come to achieve great things as a writer living in the United Kingdom, that he won the Nobel prize.

In his essay "London", Naipaul establishes clearly the reasons for his struggle for success and respectability as a writer. He culls a series of quotes from reputable reviewers of his work and determines that there is a certain cultural and nationalistic bias in their attitudes. The colonialist mentality of the British is rearing its ugly head, he suggests, though he puts it in far less polemical terms. He describes his dilemma with great lucidity. He lives in England (he had been there, at the time, for something like eight years), but he could not write about England. He did not know the English, he did not have many English friends, true friends, did not have the kind of access to the closed door of English life that he had to the inner and outer lives of Trinidadians. But he saw himself as blessed with subject matter that was fresh and rich with meaning and possibility. He had in Trinidad a group of people who lived to be characters – he did not have to make much of it up. These characters peopled his work in ways that he could not imagine that characters drawn from the British population could do. Writing about what he knew was relatively easy, and potentially rewarding, because this was fresh ground, uncharted territory. But he was faced with the danger of being seen as an exotic, a curiosity. He could tell, as early as that time, that his caustic wit, his cynical humour, and his seemingly dispassionate take on Trinidadian society would probably label him as someone who was not connected to his home land, someone hiding away in Britain, looking down his "long Oxford nose" at the poor inhabitants of his home country.

He also recognized that his approach to writing would not make him popular in other circles in Britain, for it went against the grain of how the liberal élite thought a colonial author should write. He would be better off lamenting the degradation caused by colonialism, lamenting racial discrimination or celebrating the simple beauties of the Caribbean and its people. It was evident that critics in both the Caribbean and Britain thought that what he was writing about the Caribbean was the kind of thing that only white British observers of the colonial world should have been able to do. His seeming distance from the colonial world would neither endear him to the British, nor to West Indians. Over the years, that has not changed much. The battle is no longer with Britain, but what is clear is that he is still a Trinidadian writer. This despite his knighthood won entirely as a British subject. This despite the fact that, for all intents and purposes, he has lived and worked in Britain for almost all his adult life. This despite his own seeming denial of his "Trinidadianness". He is still a Trinidadian writer, still a West Indian writer and there is little he can do to alter that.

This must be a peculiarity of Britain. I am taking a breath at this point because this is how the business with Britain comes back to me. It is almost fifty years since Naipaul wrote his essay, and one would have supposed that the concept of the immigrant British citizen would now be very different from when he started to live and work in Britain as a writer. Is it possible to be black and British, Indian and British, Chinese and British without constantly evoking a sense of one's former national identity, one's place of origin, in the discussion? Is it possible? Take someone like James Berry. He has lived in England for far longer than V.S. Naipaul. Berry arrived in Britain in the 1940s. He has never really left. Berry is, in some ways, regarded as a British writer, but then again, not really. He is decidedly a Black British writer but his Jamaicanness is constantly placed in the foreground as an integral part of what defines him. He has been placed, along with people like Archie Markham and Wilson Harris, in an echelon of elder statesmen in British letters who belong to the transcultural world – the world of the immigrant writer. What is indisputable is that Berry, according to the establishment, is not British in the way that Ted Hughes is British. One can ask whether this is a generational thing or whether writers such as Berry or Markham defined who they were by what they wrote and by the way they indeed regard themselves and speak about their work. Other questions come to mind. Did writers such as Berry position themselves as immigrants because no other option was available to them? Are things different for the younger generation of writers? Does a younger generation of critics and readers regard Linton Kwesi Johnson as being as British a writer as Andrew Motion? Has Britain changed, or have the writers themselves changed?

These days, the position of Britain's writing immigrants is far more complex than in the days of Naipaul's "London", though I see no evidence that the attitudes of the literary and publishing establishments have changed. The complication has everything to do with the fact that there are now more and more second, third and fourth generation British of African or Asian or Caribbean heritage who are now laying claim to being British. This is not just a matter of choice – a political statement – but an act of necessity. Those who were born in Britain, who have never been to or lived in Africa or the Caribbean or Asia, and who have been through a thoroughly British education, have little choice but to try to define themselves as British, or at least to evolve a category of Britishness for themselves.

For the writer in this situation, the task is challenging. The writing world is, in Britain, quite ghettoized. The Naipauls, Lammings, Soyinkas and Harrises of the world have ensured that writers of colour in Britain have to be associated not with British letters, but with an internationalist literary tradition that embraces such fields as commonwealth literature, world literature and more recently, postcolonial literature. The practice of criticism has situated itself in this paradigm and this has prompted British-born writers of colour to try to situate themselves in an immigrant sensibility and consciousness by excavating memories of origin, memories often borrowed from parents and from writers who have gone before.

The fact is that the writers who serve as models have been well ensconced in the world of the immigrant. Defining oneself as belonging to that space has been one way of trying to get some kind of critical attention. It makes things easier for the critics and reviewers. Earlier in my writing career, when most of my work was published in the UK, these issues of reception were pertinent to how I thought about my writing. But more recently, this model has been complicated for me by the introduction of America into the mix. America, you see, has a rather different attitude to the position of the black immigrant in American society. This is because there is little question about the place of blacks in American society.

What I mean by this is that unlike other non-white ethnic groups in America, the African American cannot be perceived as an alien. The African American has been here from the beginning. America, despite its efforts to erase the centrality of the African American person, is as much defined by its blackness as it is by its whiteness. The history of the black experience in America, is, in many ways, the history of America. (The same can be said about the position of the Native Americans, though that is both more fundamental and more complex because of the issues of dispossession and disenfranchisement so deeply ingrained in the Native American experience and the founding of the nation state.) But the long-standing African presence in America – for that is what it began as and what it remains – makes particular possibilities for the assimilation of immigrant blacks into American culture. The position of black people in America may not always be attractive, but the overwhelming and homogenising power of American culture consumes all with which it comes into contact, transforming it into something like belonging. There is both a tragic determinism in the inevitable liquidation of origins *and* a grand space of opportunity.

Thus, there is no such thing as a West Indian American in the sense that there are unquestionably West Indian Britons in the United Kingdom. It is not a matter of numbers; it is quite simply that those who migrated to America from the Caribbean, migrated to a society that had a slot for them, a slot that only subtly nuanced the business of difference along the lines of immigration. In time, the transplanted Caribbean person can become an African American. It is hard to resist that kind of determinism. You recognize this when you start to consider the writers from the Caribbean who live in America. While it is true that Jamaica Kincaid has been co-opted by Caribbean studies departments as a West Indian, for all intents and purposes in America, she is, quite simply, an American. Whilst her credentials as an American are not exactly borne out by the subject matter of her work, there is little else for her to be but a black American woman. There is, it is true, a slight difference in her positioning when she is placed against Maya Angelou or Alice Walker, but this is far too subtle to mean anything to the average onlooker. Most importantly, it is not enough to relegate her to being an immigrant, an exotic. She is American, as are Rosa Guy and Paule Marshall. The same can be said for Claude McKay, one of the pioneers in this business of transforming the transplanted Caribbean writer. McKay is understood as thoroughly American and his work is anthologized as an essential element of the Harlem Renaissance. There is no equivalent figure in British writing because whilst recognition of difference within the totality of America is endemic, Britain, though it holds to – and occasionally practices – attractive notions of tolerance towards the rest of the world, remains a painfully homogenous nation, quite convinced of its whiteness, its Europeanness, in a way that America may want, but is unable to manage.

This is probably why V.S. Naipaul has liked Britain. It is not that he relishes its Europeanness, but because he has always, as he says in his essays on India, enjoyed the business of being a minority – a real minority. I understand that sentiment entirely. There is something defining and reassuring about being a minority, because as a genuine minority there is little chance of being invisible. There are the advantages, too, that you are forced always to be aware of your *raison d'être*, and you are always able to distance yourself, without any sense of regret, from those things that are not good in your adopted society. Nationalism consumes the individual. Minority status often allows for distinctiveness. Needless to say, there are almost always negatives about being a minority, not least when your status is no longer salvaged by an aura of enigma and exotica, a privilege usually granted only to recently arrived minorities and rarely to minorities of long-standing residence. Long-standing minorities become written into the myths of a society, myths that are invariably negative and not, of course, usually constructed by members of the minority group.

That is why Ralph Ellison saw his minority position as an African American as akin to being invisible. He saw the black person in America as being forced into invisibility as a way of surviving the white conviction that their society was entirely a white one. Blacks belonged in the back rooms, the kitchens, the factories, the fields, and the images, the photographs that appeared in magazines, the stories told, almost always managed to make the black figure virtually nonexistent, even in places where blacks were quite significant in number. The paranoid anxiety of being overwhelmed by black society and culture created movements like the Klan or the various community organizations that sought to maintain the pre-eminence of white society and white culture (whatever that was). Invisibility in this context was necessary for one's safety, but it also offered an ambivalent space in which one could get on with one's own business.

However, the absorption of the new black immigrant to the status of honorary African American is not immediate. The moment we open our mouths, recent black immigrants are invariably asked, "Where are you from?" As soon as we name another country, somewhere outside the politics and the culture of America, somewhere outside the history of race and identity in American society, we, contrary to the assumption based on appearance, can no longer be lumped together with the native minorities. We are almost forgiven for being different.

I understand this well, because it has been part of my own experience here in America. Like many first generation West Indians and Africans in America, whites and blacks have told me that I am different, different from the African Americans who have lived here for generations. And my difference is a good difference. I am granted a certain, albeit limited, access to their thoughts and anxieties because they assume (I am here speaking largely of whites), that I do not come with the baggage carried by African Americans. They assume that I come with a fairly assured sense of identity and have no axe to grind with them as whites. This is based on the presumption that I do not carry the memory of shame or oppression that African Americans have carried in their history. They are wrong, but that is another story. Suffice to say, the immigrant in me enjoys the pathetic kind of flattery that this anomalous position encourages. It reminds me of my difference, helps me to cope with the alienation I feel, and indulges my nostalgia for home. It gives me permission to say certain things and get away with them. I have to resist it. But I understand what it is all about and I have learnt a great deal from being in this position. I have been able to hear whites talk about African Americans in ways that they admit they would not do in their company because, according to the whites, African Americans will not listen. What the whites do not say is that they are reluctant to talk openly to African Americans because of their feelings of guilt or their feelings of resentment over the suggestion that they should feel guilty. They will admit their sense of guilt to me, the alien, but they are less willing to do so in front of African Americans.

This is an intense battle, a battle involving deepest emotions. There is power in the ability to hold someone responsible for the condition of your life. There is much that needs to be written about the power of guilt and the weight of penitence in the politics of racial relationships. For a white person to admit some culpability in the race problem means conceding that there is something fundamentally wrong with the society and, further, it means giving ground to the African Americans who have been saying this for years. Whites, even when they are penitent, when they regret the problems that their ancestors caused, will not admit this readily because it would mean conceding something to black people, whom they do not regard as entirely blameless. They are not willing to concede that African Americans have always been wronged. They are not willing to concede anything that will make them vulnerable. It is warfare and the access that I am allowed to the combatants sometimes makes me feel like a very privileged reporter who has been allowed into the war rooms of the opposing sides.

As an immigrant I have certain privileges. But I am aware that I am no normal immigrant. There are many immigrants who have had tidy and restrictive slots established for them in various cities in the country. These slots are totalizing and ghettoizing: the Mexicans in Chicago and California, the Puerto Ricans and Haitians in New York, and the Cubans in Miami. And even as these boxes are created, the whites complain that the immigrants will not assimilate, will not learn the language, will not try to be American, accept American values. Those immigrant groups have no real privileges and many disadvantages, but they are aware of one thing: that they have a sense of purpose, an angst, a context in American society, which in many ways, is what living in America is all about.

And here some confession is useful. As I have admitted earlier, I enjoy being different in America because it helps me to cope with the vestigial guilt of being co-opted into a capitalist system

– the aftereffects of the value system that was instilled in me by not so subtle paternal ways during my 'socialist' childhood. I like to feel that I have not been entirely co-opted, despite the fact that I clearly have been. The system consumes you, first with debt, and then with its seductive capacity to make you feel comfortable.

A related confession is concerned with the issue of origins. Naipaul describes the East Indian in the West Indies as a fraud, because he understands that he is not a 'real' Indian and as such has to exist with a fraudulent sense of self. He suggests that all immigrants are frauds after a while, particularly those who keep reminding the host society that they have a place of origin that they are still connected to, that still defines them. The fraud lies in the fact that the connection is to a myth. The longer you are away from the world of origins, the more fraudulent, according to Naipaul, is your claim to connection. The Indians in Trinidad, he argues, have no idea what India is really like and are connected to a myth. They may claim to be from India but they are aliens in India. He would say the same about African Americans who claim a connection with Africa. They are connecting to a myth, a myth that has been fed through films such as *Roots* and through the elaborate quasi-historical texts that limit Africa to Egypt and the pyramids and the like. Naipaul would probably argue that the business of being Italian American or Irish American is fraudulent too, one of the tricks of being an immigrant, a trick used to ensure a sense of difference, identity and sometimes political advantage. The problem with Naipaul's assertion is that he does not go far enough, to say that all nationality is fraudulent. If he would admit that, then we could begin from the premise that we are all frauds trying to make the most of our lives.

My fraudulence, though, has a peculiar and sometimes confusing complexity. Ghanaian by birth, Jamaican by upbringing, with significant sojourns in the UK and Canada, and now an established resident of Columbia, South Carolina, I have to admit that this nomadic quality in my life – an ambivalent one because I have the strange and disturbing habit of allowing fresh roots to sprout from my body and cling tenaciously to the soil of any new place, regardless of how barren and unwelcoming – may prove to be my undoing as a writer. So far it has not helped much with my poetry. I am not American enough to be published by an American publisher, or foreign enough to be picked up by those US presses that like to explore the world outside this continent. On the other hand, I am not British enough to enter the echelons of the British poetry world, nor am I American enough to get into the space reserved for a sampling of American poets in the UK. I am not famous enough to be completely embraced as Jamaican by the Caribbean, and my writing is certainly not even remotely Ghanaian enough to have me read as an African author. It is possible, though, that if I keep repeating this litany and chanting the almost lyrical mantra of my origins and movements to enough people, I will be seen as a sufficiently curious specimen to be marketable as a transcultural freak. This may be my future.

What I am working on now, with some success, is mastering my various accents. This may get me through. I have a fairly good Ghanaian accent that I have to put on when I call the Ghanaian embassy, otherwise they will hang up on me, after promptly, and somewhat impatiently, giving me the number for the Guyanese Embassy.

"This is the Ghana embassy, sah!"

"Yes, I know, I want the Ghana embassy."

"The Guyanese embassy's number is..."

"No, I want the Ghana embassy, I need a passport..."

"Oh, but you can't get a passport from us. Do you have a Guyanese passport now?"

"I have a Ghanaian passport..."

"Well, I am looking for the number for the Guyanese Embassy... Please hold on a minute...."

"I don't need the Guyanese Embassy..."

At which point I slip into thick Ghanaian English and all is well. We laugh about fufu, about banku, about the hardship of living in this country and such niceties. These days I assume accents quite quickly. In England I have a bastardized Oxford lilt (which I stole from my father) which makes me sound somewhat foreign, but it becomes hard to distinguish me from an educated West Indian, or Indian or Pakistani Britisher. I have developed a few East End aphorisms that I imagine lubricate my movements around London. There are moments when a thick, very thick, Jamaican accent becomes apropos – particularly when I am performing in very dub venues and I have to boast my credentials. I have also developed a fairly good Southern accent, which is handy when I am trying to do business here or when I am calling from outside the States. It has enough of a Jamaican tinge to make folk at the other end of the line sufficiently curious to ask about my wonderful accent. I don't mind; it gets me in. Finally, in countries hostile to America, I simply moderate the Americanisms and am quite easily mistaken for an immigrant to Canada. I play all of these with disturbing ease. I am a pathetic chameleon constantly engaged in a game of mimicry: in short, a fraud.

The deception, though, does not always go unpunished. It is a given that writers are defined by their nationality. The universities teach literature according to national cultures; anthologies tend to be defined by similar considerations; and awards are often given as an accolade for representation, and representation usually takes us back to nationality in some way.

In 2004, I received a call telling me I had been shortlisted for the Commonwealth Writers Prize for my short story collection, *A Place to Hide*. I was elated. The book, I was told, was one of four finalists from the Caribbean/Canadian region.

The winner of that regional prize would go on to compete with the rest of the world for the coveted overall prize. I was proud of this achievement and quickly assumed that things would go no further. A few weeks later I discovered that the book had won the regional prize and was now among four shortlisted for the final prize. At this point, my routine pessimism kicked in. There had to be a catch. So I went to the web site to look at the rules. There was a catch. I did not qualify. I was not eligible to have won in this regional category. It was laid out in plain English. The winner had to be a citizen of the region in which they were competing. An honest error had been made. My publishers, assuming that I held dual citizenship between Ghana and Jamaica, and knowing the work, like most of my work, to be wholly Jamaican, had entered me as a Jamaican. A gracious withdrawal had to be made. It was a painful lesson in the complexities of nationality and identity, and the anomalies involved in living in America, writing about Jamaica and being published in the UK.

CHAPTER 7

why i am still a ghanaian

This business of nationality – Ghanaian passport, Jamaican sensibility – takes on a particular complexity in a country as patriotic and nationalistic as America.

There are the simple pragmatics of dealing with conversational enquiries. Thus, whenever anyone asks me where I am from, I quickly say, 'Jamaica.' It is easier. Saying 'Ghana' tends to confuse what they assumed was an easy placing of accent. But I also say Jamaica because it remains my immediate frame of reference when I talk of home.

Then there is the matter of dealing with the American assumption that people from elsewhere in the world would dearly love to be in the USA. Telling people I am from Jamaica helps to deflect the inevitably uncomfortable debate around this issue. Jamaica means something largely positive to Americans. They are willing to entertain the idea that I would want to return there to enjoy the beaches, the sun and all that culture. I am not an easy charity case as a Jamaican. Many Americans have been to Jamaica, and in some ways regard it as an US outpost. Despite this, I still find myself in conversations that seem intent on pushing me to the place where I am supposed to say, 'Thank God, I came to America.' When I declare my Ghanaianess, this pressure is even greater.

It is greater not least because my claim to being Ghanaian is tenuous. I realize this when I find myself needing to have my Ghanaianness validated by other Ghanaians. The defining factor is language. Without it, one feels like a fraud. It is true that sometimes there is recognition, the feeling that when you hear the language, you know it in a strange kind of way. But that sense of illusory connection doesn't last long. When you are asked about Ghana, you have to rely on the selective and much reshaped memories you have stored in your imagination, memories which, in any case, are dated and don't reflect the Ghana of today; or you have to rely on what you have read in newspapers, magazines, or on news from relatives. But you have to recognize right away that you are making much of it up. It is hard to say that you just don't know, that you have not been there for decades, and that the current world is no longer the world of your origins. That admission is most disturbing. On the one hand, in some circles in America these days, in the currency of blackness there is no better credential than to be actually from Africa. It means that you are authentic, that your name was not something you acquired in adult years. To have to admit that you, too, are a bit of a fraud, is hard. On the other hand, to espouse my Ghanaianness in other American contexts, where Africa has become a byword for human calamities and the failed nation state, has few rewards.

Of course, I can't just dismiss my Ghanaianness in this way. To call it a fraud is flippant, and evades the greater truth is that all nationalism is fraudulent in the face of the human and cultural connections that are unwilling to respect the borders of the nationalisms we create. But there are for me (as no doubt for many others sceptical about nationalism), still deep emotional connections that are impossible to dismiss. Even so, I only retrieve Ghana as a commitment to nation when there is a soccer game involving Ghana or a Ghanaian is competing in a race at the Olympics. These are rare moments. What is more common is finding myself engaged in trying to understand myself as someone shaped by a history somewhat removed from the history of the people around me. My reconstruction of Ghana is inevitably subjective and closer to fiction – the fiction of memory – than it is to historical recollection. I was too young for anything else to be the case. But I still feel rooted there at some profound and meaningful level. Maybe this feeling is about coping with the rootlessness of not being there. Yet were I to live in Ghana now, I would probably not feel rooted.

But, however meaningful, I know that my Ghanaianness is tenuous because I have not yet found the language with which to communicate the colour and taste of my connection to my children. The truth is that there is little that I have to offer, little that I have at my fingertips. I could ensure that when they enter a room full of people, they will go around and shake each person's hand politely. I had to do that as a child and it taught me respect. I have not imposed that on them as yet and I am sorry for not doing so. I could start cooking more Ghanaian dishes, but that would smack of the superficial and pretentious – and anyway, I am not sure anyone else would eat these meals. We could take a trip to Ghana, an expensive proposition which would, most likely, become a tourist excursion. For my wife and children it would be exactly that. Still we try. We talk of Ghana as a place of origin. We speak of the beauty and the hardship of the entire African continent, and we try to battle the notions of Africa that permeate American society. And we rely on their grandmother's retrieval of Ghana when she is with us.

This is in marked contrast to the children's sense of connection to Jamaica. From the beginnings of their lives they paid little or no attention to stories or recordings specifically made for children, or the very high-pitched songs that children are supposed to like. They preferred Bob Marley, Paul Simon, and anything with a reggae back-beat or some kind of African styling thrown into the mix. I am not making this up – nor am I trying to suggest that this interest has not been nurtured by their parents. We forced them to hear this stuff in-utero. We parents like to leave some kind of legacy in our children and the small window of opportunity for that is when children can't really argue.

Sena, the eldest, must have heard every one of my band Ujamaa's live performances when she was still in Lorna's womb, just as Kekeli listened to the recorded CD of the band and the music of the Marley clan, (especially Ziggy Marley) and Burning Spear (all popular in my home during the year of his gestation). He came out skanking and chatting up a storm about Marcus Garvey. Most were puzzled; we were not. Akua listened to Lucky Dube, to Paul Simon's album, *Rhythm of the Saints*, and several compilations of music by Marley. She must have come out dancing to UB40s latest album of that time, a big favourite in the house while she was taking shape. So it is our fault and while we tried to play more classical stuff and a great deal more jazz (which they seem to like), we were stuck with reggae children. They understood the off-beat of the skank, and trust me when I say that watching that happen was more exciting than watching them start to walk or talk. I mean this. These were the ways in which we tried to inculcate a sense of cultural difference in the children. It would destroy me if my children were to declare one day (as I am certain they will – I am pessimistic that way) that they hate reggae music. This thought terrifies me. It would mean that their most crucial evidence of difference would have gone. I am gratified that right now they like reggae. It means they are connected to Jamaica, even if they have only visited that country a few times.

As my books, *Bob Marley: Lyrical Genius* and *Natural Mysticism* make plain, Reggae is important to me. I regard it as a defining source of nostalgia and a grounding in terms of my understanding of home. I am inscribed in reggae and reggae permeates all that

I write and all that I think about artistic expression and aesthetics. When I was writing *Natural Mysticism*, I recognized a beginning of my own sense of identity and cultural definition around the age of ten or eleven. This was in the period after I arrived in Jamaica and began to learn Jamaica's culture and language. It is not entirely a true construct because, in hindsight, what I actually did when I was thinking about and writing *Natural Mysticism* was to fall into amnesia about the relationship between myself and Ghana. It was not a conscious amnesia, but it remained with me for a long time and has only recently begun to crumble away in strange and curious ways. While in Jamaica, as I have said, I always regarded Ghana as my home and Ghana as the source of my sense of culture and cultural values. My nostalgic sensibility was focused on Ghana. Ghanaian landscapes, memories, sounds and voices were powerful and defining. They differentiated me from the Jamaican world. I had recognized some basic cultural differences between Ghana and Jamaica early on in my life in Jamaica.

There were the attitudes to violence and the spectacle of death. I could not understand the propensity to violence so endemic in the Jamaican psyche. I was always struck by it: the fights in the school yard, the stone wars – boys and girls playing a game of flinging stones at each other, quite committed to the business of causing serious bodily harm as if this was fun – and the tendency of people to gravitate towards trouble, towards the prospect and spectacle of violence or death. Where I would instinctively turn away from crowds gathered around a car accident, Jamaicans would run towards it. I found all these things to be quite contrary to my basic instincts and I understood them to be culturally defined. Even now, it is hard to explain why I perceived these things to be matters of cultural difference but, in my gut, I understood them in those terms.

There were other basic differences: differences in our attitudes towards Africa and blackness. As I have written earlier, I understood Africa as home while many Jamaicans were deeply ambivalent about Africa. But when I left Jamaica, I left largely as a Jamaican. It was harder to explain that I was African, that I was Ghanaian, because everything about me pointed to Jamaica – everything on the surface that is. By the time of my third removal – to the United States, after Canada – I was holding on to Jamaica with greater ferocity than I was holding on to Ghana. Perhaps this was because Ghana was a given, a part of me that was locked in childhood memory, whereas as an adult I was deeply inscribed in my Jamaicanness.

But just recently, I experienced a feeling of connection to Ghana that moved me in a way that few things have moved me in a long time. The experience did not totally eclipse my sense of being a fraud, but it did remind me why I am a Ghanaian in spite of myself. It reminded me that my mother's Ghanaianness holds far more weight than I have been acknowledging up to this point, where I have been mostly exploring my father's influence on me. But the truth is I am terribly close to my mother, and her assumption of my Ghanaianness is a given. There is no discussion about that at all. I have clear links through blood, ties as ancient as her memories. Ghana, then, is a real part of my construction of a sense of home and consequently I feel it must become the same for my children. I have cousins, perhaps hundreds of them, living in Ghana today. My children have relatives in Cape Coast, Lome, Tema, Kumasi, and Accra. Maybe one day they will meet them, or perhaps they won't, but they have a link with Ghana that they cannot easily ignore because, despite the immediacy of Jamaica, we have far more relatives, on my side, living in Ghana than we do in Jamaica. There are such actual family connections and then there is the strange emotional connection that recently so moved me.

I was driving the family back from Sumter, through the police-infested swamp highway 378; everyone in the car had fallen asleep. It was a brilliant day, with the kind of true light that I relish driving in. The car was now silent after the tape that had been playing during the trip down had come to an end. It was a poorly recorded but disturbingly catchy series of Christian reggae gospel tunes by a band, Birthright, a group of contemporaries and friends of Lorna and I when we were undergraduates in Jamaica in the early eighties. I quickly punched it out of the cassette player before the auto-reverse could kick into gear. I did it with some trepidation because my children had the uncanny habit of waking and demanding music when they were disturbed from deep sleep. They stayed quiet this time. The silence was good, but I gradually became tired of that as well. I tried the radio and listened to it speed from one station to the other without settling anywhere. When it settled for a minute, the music was annoyingly operatic. Another time, another place. So I foraged through the cassettes on the car floor and I found a caseless tape by a group called Abundant Life. It was one of Lorna's tapes from London and it contained music by a Ghanaian gospel group she had seen when she was living there in the eighties. She had told me about the group and how much she liked it.

At the time, Lorna was seriously considering the prospect of marrying me, a Ghanaian. All this confirms that while I was in Jamaica (where we met), I was very clear about my Ghanaianness. I know that the food I liked to eat was Ghanaian and I tried to learn to cook banku and okra and all that kind of stuff. Lorna had met my mother and this must have reinforced her perception that much of my defining sense of self was rooted in Ghana. So while she was in London, Lorna started to do some research or preparation for marriage to a Ghanaian. I found this flattering but a bit misguided for, by this time, when I was in Canada, I was very acutely aware of my Jamaicanness. (It later became clear that her activities were less about getting to know my culture and more that she was enjoying the Ghanaian connection for its own sake.) She took drumming lessons from

113

a Ghanaian and travelled around London buying carvings and cloth in stores run by Ghanaians. She had concluded that while the cultures (Jamaican and Ghanaian) were different, she liked Ghanaians – for some interesting reasons. I had my ideas, but it would have been vain and nationalistic to offer them. So when she saw this group, Abundant Life, in performance, she was impressed by their dancing, their force of character, their witness and their willingness to enjoy their faith in the context of their culture. There was none of the awkwardness of Jamaican Christians trying to play reggae and going through the struggle of justifying such an act, as was the case in the 1980s before the churches gingerly embraced reggae music.

I put the tape into the slot and listened, at first casually, half-expecting the tape to be warped and completely useless (a condition true of fifty percent of the tapes in the car).

The music engulfed and transported me.

There is no other way to describe what happened. It was by no means an unfamiliar feeling, yet it still felt an uniquely powerful one, a revelation. It is curious how music can simultaneously affect one's psyche and one's body. My stomach became uneasy – an excitability that has always accompanied the deep, seemingly sorrow-like symptoms of nostalgia. It was some time before I consciously recognised that this syncopated music – high life – this sound of voices speaking a language that I 'understood' in strangely intuitive ways – not word-by-word, but movement-by-movement, sentiment-by-sentiment – had completely captured me and forced me to travel into a memory as old as childhood. At that visceral level, it is impossible to put into words the processes that go into this shaping of identity and memory. There is nothing coherent, just fragments of images that spring into the imagination. I am always tempted to try to analyse these fragments, place them in some kind of intellectual context, which is, of course, the business of prose. This moment was like a poem, not a successful and completed poem, but the poem you attempt again and again, but always arrive at something that seems deeply prosaic, completely inadequate to the feeling filling your mind and body. This is what it felt like. I wanted to halt the moment, stop the car to try and write it down, but the more I thought about writing it, the more I realized that I would not know what to write. I was not in a particular place, I was not thinking of any moment recoverable to memory; I was in a space of nostalgic recollection, of transported feelings and sentiment.

I allowed my mind to travel and started to consider the images that entered my head as I manoeuvred the vehicle along the 378. The memories came in snippets, tiny bits – of another long ride, but this time along a curvy hilly road, below us, at each bend, the rocky ravine and a massive river – rugged, angry and speedy – like nothing I had seen in Jamaica, though the heat was the same. The landscape was different, stonier, the boulders larger, the road wider. The music took me there, inside a Rover three litre. I have no idea where we were going to or coming from. I just remember the ride, and this music took me there. Then it took me to a Trade Fair. That is what we called it. I recall that the Trade Fair was in Tema somewhere, and that we would put on swimsuits and play in a fountain that I am not sure was designed for swimming. The swimming, the screaming of children, warm roasted nuts, the fried corn balls called *akra*, and afterwards the fried and peppery plantains called *kelewele*: these things came back as I listened to the music. I recalled the walk home through the bushes, the fear of snakes, the way that sunset would suggest itself, red and amazingly powerful along the flatlands of Accra, broken only by the sentinel anthills of our private savanna. I recalled the night walks that we would make as children of several families, walking through Legon's residential area, laughing, stopping at the heavily vined lattice work of the front porch of a couple – the woman Japanese and the man Ghanaian – who lived in Legon. The house was always lit with oriental bamboo lamps that marked the walkway to the ornamented front door. There were white statues scattered all over the garden, and the light from inside the house would glow through the muted shapes of the Japanese characters and the images of kimonoed Japanese women shuffling as if suspended in air. This image is not grounded in any specific memory, but I recalled that there was this couple and this house. The music evoked them. The music evoked the twenty-minute drive from Legon to Achimota where we first lived and the stop by the lamp-lit roadside vendors who sold nuts and *kelewele* wrapped in greasy newspapers. We would eat this rich meal while driving to the Senior Common room where my father would join his cronies and drink, while we ate groundnuts and sometimes very thickly onioned (fried sweet onions) hamburgers served in grease-proof paper. As I drove along the 378, I realized that I was looking into a memory that had not yet begun to permeate my poetry. I found it fascinating that I would begin in Jamaica and then make my way back. The memories, even as I write this, are growing in my mind: rich, moving recollections of death, life, fear, happiness, anxiety and the brilliance of humour. The truth of it all is that Ghana was a shaping place for me, and I am only now starting to tap into what that means.

Lorna woke and asked me where I had found the tape. I laughed and said I had placed it in the car a long time ago, hoping to play it. I started to talk about the impact the music was having on me. She did not seem surprised, simply smiled in acknowledgment at what should have been patently obvious to me: that my sense of self is contained in the meaning of my experiences in Ghana. The stories of my childhood, the ones that as a family we have passed from one to the other – told again and again – are the things that have shaped my instinct as a storyteller. I am full of stories because I came from a home in which story-making was basic to our existence. It strikes me as a truly African quality. Indeed, the way that memory has taken shape in my mind these days has been through these stories.

Next morning, I got a call from my mother. She was in Trinidad with a group of childhood friends of ours, people I had not seen for a couple of decades. We talked and all of that remembering while listening to Abundant Life came to a head in this conversation. My mother was crying and when Uncle Benji, a dear friend of my late father, came on the phone, he could only say, "Chochoo [my mother] has made me the happiest I have been in years. I am now a happy man. A happy man. I can't say anything because I am crying. Kwame, Kwame, kiss the children for me." I think I understood the moment completely. He was not simply enjoying the pleasure of this moment of meeting again, but he was remembering me as a child, remembering the closeness we all shared as families in Accra, remembering my father and the loss of his friend, and perhaps hearing my father in me. It was a touching moment for all of us. Even though this call came from Trinidad where this family, the Thompsons, had moved several years ago, I think that in that moment, they too were drawing on the memory of Ghana, the memory of Legon, and the smell and taste of that landscape.

It is clear that in all that I have written about these memories, there is little that is tangible or coherent. Indeed, much of what has been evoked in this journey into memory has been transient. I would probably not see any of these things were I to return to Ghana today. But the very nebulousness of such memories represents the deep, essential core of nostalgia. There are, though, other sources of connection that I am sure would withstand the shock and euphoria of a visit to Ghana. I would return to the home of my grandfather and the home of my grandmother – that circular compound with the mound of heat-toughened mud in the middle where she baked bread – in that village in Cape Coast where she used to let us run wild among the fishermen and the farmers; I would find the graves that hold their bodies and the bodies of all my other relatives and my ancestors. I know I would connect to these people, an ancient people, who are part of my defining. That land is the space I grew out of, and one day I will make a connection to it that goes beyond nostalgia. But in the mean time, nostalgia will shore up my memory and keep awake my sense of Ghana.

I am, despite the slippery nature of my Ghanaianness, as I hinted at earlier in the chapter, in an interesting position as an African in America. For many African Americans, my Ghanaian nationality represents physical evidence of their ancestry, a complicated and sometimes ambivalent connection to the tenuous past. During the 1950s and 1960s, a significant number of African Americans (and Caribbean Blacks – including my father) travelled to Ghana to live out the ideals of Pan-Africanism. For many of them, Africa, and Ghana in particular, was seen as a genuine alternative to their lives in America. They felt that ideologically, culturally and socially, it was a better place to be than America. They wanted to be part of developing that society. Idealism, yes, but a compelling idealism. For many of that generation, I am a brother. But for a younger generation, I come from a place that is a cipher for failed nationalist dreams, a place that is still located in many American minds, black and white, as part of a dark, uncertain continent. This Africa cannot be home.

Quite recently, a television show made clear for me how Americans wrestle with the idea of Africa. This was a late show in which a quite funny and outspoken host invited people of diverse backgrounds, but with the common ability to be outrageous or controversial, to talk on air. On this particular show, which turned to the issue of race, the host declared, with no small glee, that a Black scholar had confessed in one of his books that, in his heart of hearts, he was grateful his ancestors had been wrenched from Africa and placed here in America;

that when he compared his life here to the lives of Africans, he was grateful to have been a "victim" of the slave trade. The talk-show host was probably quoting this author out of context, but the relish with which he did so was telling. It is not uncommon for white people to remind blacks that they should be grateful for the slave trade because it rescued them from the current woes of African life. They point to Rwanda, to Sudan, to Zaire, to Zimbabwe, to Liberia, to Ethiopia and they say, "Now think, do you really mean that you would prefer to be there than here in America? You must be kidding." The subtext is a twisted attempt by some whites to exonerate themselves from their complicity in not questioning the social order bequeathed by slavery. There is also the suggestion that black societies need to be rescued by white influence. Another person on the same show declared that: "Africa was better off under colonialism than it is now. The colonial times did good things for Africa." It is not difficult to take apart the idiocy of these articulations and the misguidedness of their assumptions. This has been done by others before me. But I have the feeling that it is increasingly necessary to tackle these simple-minded but dangerous arguments every time they emerge.

Was it simple ignorance that allowed people like the talk-show host to fail to recognize that the state of Africa is inextricably linked to the tragedy of the slave trade, the imposed and heterogeneous nation states imposed by European colonialism, the terms of global trade so unfairly stacked against primary producers, or the subversive activities of pre-liberation South Africa? Was it simple naiveté that allowed our talk-show host to assume that material wealth is everything that defines a sense of national identity and national pride? Was it naiveté that allowed him to ignore the reality that not all the people living in Africa are fighting to move to America and that, if they are, they are not doing so in order to become Americans but as a means of securing a share of the wealth that America (and Europe) has sucked out of their continent? Was it ignorance that prevented him from wondering whether those Africans who were brought here – the millions who lived on the plantations (and the millions who died in the middle passage) – really did prefer being in America, really did prefer being slaves to being free in their own lands? Was it naiveté that stopped him thinking that if African Americans no longer wanted to return to Africa, it was becuse slavery had destroyed their capacity to belong to their original communities, and because American-born Africans knew no other place than America. Was it naiveté that made him fail to recognize that at the heart of the black scholar's confession was a callous selfishness, and that his appropriation of this selfishness had dehumanized slavery so that it became not a true narrative of the suffering of real people, but a myth of arrival to be appropriated whenever necessary and forgotten just as readily? For what was it other than selfishness that allowed the scholar to conclude that his ancestors' suffering was worth it because of what he now had? Would his ancestors agree? Would they regard the condition of the generality of blacks in this society as something that was worth all that they had gone through?

I am not suggesting that slavery did not benefit some Africans – I am sure it did, nor am I denying that a minority of African Americans have gained access to the "good things" of American life, nor am I saying – and this is even more crucial – that African Americans haven't created something of immense and heroic value in the USA. But one can also argue that the creation of the state of Israel was one consequence of the Holocaust, and there was no doubt a very small minority of Jews who benefited in more direct ways, but does that, in any way, allow me to feel that Jewish people should be grateful for the Holocaust? Would our talk-show host offer that as a subject for debate, or is that far too sensitive even for the profitable business of politically incorrect discourse?

As a Ghanaian living in the United States, I don't regard myself as especially grateful to be here. Does this mean that I must regard myself as participating in a game of ingratitude? No. That is the wrong question to ask. America is a great country, but I have not buried anything that connects me spiritually to this land. I have no nostalgic connections to this landscape and to this language. It may come in time, but at the moment, I cannot deny my connections beyond these borders. I live here, I work here, and I contribute here because I have come to learn that becoming a part of a community is part of what it means to be human.

Yet, as I have begun to suggest, over time a sense of connection to this country began. It happened in small ways. I was quicker to embrace my South Carolinianess than any wider Americanness. When I leave South Carolina, people tend to have views about the state that are based on ignorance or arrogance that I find wholly familiar. I feel the need to defend my friends, to defend the state and what I know of its history and culture. I have developed for South Carolina that attitude one has for family. It is fine for me to speak ill of the place, but for strangers to do so... I know this feeling is absurd. South Carolinians don't regard me as one of them, despite my having lived here for fourteen years. But there is a greater sense of affinity between us than there was ten years ago, or five years ago, for that matter. What is at the heart of this feeling of connection is, I believe, the substantial African American presence in the history of South Carolina. As I have indicated earlier, I remain shaped by my deeply emotional and visceral reaction to the details of trans-Atlantic slavery. So South Carolina's narrative of slavery, its history of segregation and the horrors of Jim Crow all feel like my story. This is why I find myself at home in the South: this is a place for my kind that goes back for centuries. Shared suffering and struggle is no small force.

Maybe it has been living in South Carolina with its depth of African presence that reinforced my sense of connection to Ghana. But the truth is mine is not a quest for nation – indeed, I am far more interested in how nationalism finds me.

The thing that probably allows me to confess my Ghanaianess without feeling like a fraud is the embrace of Ghanaians who have no sense of distance from their national and ethnic roots. Being Ghanaian connects me to my mother and my relatives in significant ways. I wouldn't call it pride, although there is pride involved, but I would call it an assurance of belonging which, ultimately, is more useful to me.

Here in the USA, my wish is that my connection to Africa is respected and sometimes celebrated. It is neither a simple connection, nor one that resides only in myth, but one that is potentially the same even for those who have been several generations removed from Africa. The recovery of our history is a powerful source of dignity and self-definition that we cannot ignore, dismiss or allow amnesia to bury.

CHAPTER 8

a man among real men

It should be clear by now that my entire sense of self, my position as a Ghanaian living in America, having lived in Jamaica somewhere in between, is defined by my relationship with my father. My very fatherhood, my relationships with women and men, my understanding of my class values, my art, my profession, are all in some way connected to my father. I spend a good deal of time evaluating the details of my life in the light of my memory of him.

On the surface, my father's legacy does not appear very tangible.

He did not leave us a home or any real estate. During the madness of the flight of the upper-middle class from Jamaica to Miami or Canada in the seventies, we had a chance to buy the large house we were renting on Carlisle Avenue. The owners were willing to sell it at a reasonable price. My mother was keen; she wanted us to go ahead, but my father said no. He was a Marxist and home ownership was too bourgeois. At the time, he had a good job. Perhaps he had anticipated the loss of his job and the prospect of a large mortgage seemed like a nightmare to him. In any event, we did not buy the home and we were soon evicted from it when the owners, who had fled the spectre of imminent revolution, began to think of returning. When my father did eventually lose his job, there began a nomadic movement from one house to another as rents proved too much (the places getting smaller and smaller each time).

There was a property we were supposed to own a share of in Sturge Town, tucked into the hills of St. Ann's. My father made a half-hearted gesture of interest in the property to the people who now lived on the land. They were not going anywhere. My father gave up. The property is still there. It seems so far away now. A more aggressive family would have fought for their share of that land, but tellingly, I have no interest in such efforts. The land feels like someone else's. I'm no doubt wrong in this matter, but such is the nature of my father's legacy.

My father did not leave any other kind of inheritance. We expected this, yet we went through his papers in search of hidden treasures. He left my mother a good deal of debt, which took years to clear up. It may have been irresponsibility; the truth is that my father was too generous. He did not, though, spend much on himself. His only indulgence was books and, even then, he did not buy that many, as many were sent to him by fellow writers. His legacy was the library of books: thousands of titles and a remarkable West Indian Literature collection. But it was not cash and we needed cash. What he had left with us was a very distinct attitude to money: it was to be spent – spent on making life meaningful. It was not something to pursue for its own sake and being smart with money was nothing to celebrate. He never said this to us in so many words, but he lived it. We all followed suit. Three of us became teachers because we love teaching. One of us is an artist and the other is a civil servant. We could have been more ambitious, but it was not in us to be that way. We had not learned the sterner stuff of individual ambition. In this was something of the logic of his socialist creed.

I grew up with a rather unsophisticated model of utopia: unsophisticated because it grew out of the fundamental premise that society should sacrifice to create fairness – equality was the ideal. So I struggled with Plato's elevation of the philosopher to a place of inalienable privilege; it did not seem like cricket. At school, I was embarrassed by my desire to be in the A stream and the secret pride I felt about being among the brightest in my class. I could not accept the notion that I came from a middle class home or that my father was part of the Jamaican intelligentsia. These things would make me feel better than someone else and that was bourgeois and quite sickening. In truth, my upbringing was not a materially rich one, for we always knew there was no permanence to any of it. We knew that none of us would be walking into an inheritance at any point, as many of my schoolmates would. And yet, part of my definition of self was, fundamentally, an act of denial. Privilege was not cool and I spent a great deal of time boasting about my poverty. It was sometimes absurd, but it points to the kind of value system that I inherited. So he left neither wealth nor a desire for wealth.

I have had to learn how to handle money, how to make the business of making good money a priority. I had to learn the hustle of self-promotion that is basic to American life. The whole business of negotiating salaries, demanding fees for artistic performances, considering financial options about buying property and insurance, thinking of ways to make more: these were the things I had to contend with in America. America changed me. This became clear when, in 1995, I came to England to promote my poetry. I realized that in two years of living in America, I had grown accustomed to self-promotion as not just legitimate, but as a sign of confidence and ability. I had to relearn the very British practice of third-party commendation, and the wearying, but deeply mannered practice of self-depreciation, of dishonest self-denial. Ignore this veneer of false modesty at the risk of hubristic destruction!

My father's Marxism was thoroughgoing and the only useful

comparison would be with my Christianity. Indeed, my embrace of Christianity was as heady and radical as my father's Marxism was for him in his twenties. Passion drove him. He wrote his novels and poems struggling to make them relevant to his political vision, part of a struggle he was willing to contemplate dying for. I spent my time as an undergraduate at UWI trying to shape an aesthetic for Christian drama. I was also willing to die for my faith.

But my Christianity, while emerging in the ideologically volatile late 1970s, did not arrive as a counter to my father's Marxism. In fact, I never found the two ideas to be really so opposed. I was comfortable with the notion that a complete dismissal of God was not absolutely essential to the embrace of socialist ideals. However, my Christianity arrived as a very personal response to the basic questions of mortality, morality and the supernatural. I became a Christian because I met the message and person of Christ in a crisis of spiritual and psychic upheaval. I cannot alter the palpable force of that encounter. It would come to define me. I was radically Christian.

My father's sense of fair play was Marxist. Mine was not rooted in the study of Marxism. I simply inherited it as one does good manners and it shaped my attitude to sports, to academia, to relationships, and to my faith. The deeply competitive and material nature of much of American Christianity, which sees wealth as a blessing from God (an eloquent rationalization of power and privilege that is quite decadent) remains a problem for me because of this vague, but very persistent socialist principle I got from my father.

My father did not leave the great novel he said he was writing. We thought he would have left something: an outline, even. But there was nothing. We went through his papers, boxes of papers – at least those we could find. No manuscript, but we found letters, we found traces of his more silent self in the confessions of his letters and the dialogue he had with friends and family. It was clear that he wanted to write that great novel. He had written two novels in twenty years. He wrote well, wrote sophisticated and always intelligent prose that managed to marry sensuality with intellect in the most natural way. But his desire to write the next great book was a dream. And hard as it is to admit this, I think my father stopped writing because of us, because of his children. It is not so much that we got in his way or became a burden on him, but that he became comfortable, that he found satisfaction in being a father. The peculiar restlessness that drives most writers can grow mute when there is a degree of peace, a stability that ironically has been longed for. My mother was his stability and we children were his crafted things. In our younger days, he would, while under his waters, call us out of sleep and line us up. He would sit and smile and begin to count from the oldest to the youngest: "One, two, three, four, five. All present and accounted for. My poems. My poems." At three o'clock in the morning we did not feel much like reading love into that annoyance, but this is what it was.

He had stopped writing poems just about the time we were coming into this world. I realized something about him when I contemplated his literary legacy. It was modest, but inch space was not what drove him forward. Above all, his passion was to make others shine, to help others, to celebrate others, to establish a pattern of valuing others. This is what drew all the writers who found refuge from the chaos of their lives in our home. Neville's life was stable among writers who were often far from stable. He must have decided that his family life was enough for him. But you could tell that he also felt a sense of loss, a sense of not having quite fulfilled his promise, his talent, his genius. It would come out in his claim to be writing this great book, this novel that never materialized. I know it was all in his head, all turning in his head. He just had not written it down. It is a trait he left me: this capacity to construct a piece of work in the mind, making the process of writing it down a fast, driven act of some tedium, the mind tumbling ahead of the pen. So he left no book, but what he left me was a model of being a "normal" artist, a "normal" poet, unimpressed with any mystique about what is just a craft. It may be cynicism, but I am never able to call myself a poet and imagine it to be even remotely romantic.

There is much in what I have to say in this book that would give the impression that I have placed my father as the most important figure in my life. In truth, this is an overstatement or, more simply, a falsehood. My mother's legacy is equally powerful if not more so. But I find myself at this point trying to fathom the business of self through the dynamic relationship of fathers and sons.

To understand what it means for me to live and work in America, it is absolutely essential to understand my father and his thoughts about America. I carry in me a constant dialogue, an argument almost, that is pitched between us. There is in this dialogue much that relates to the larger issues of what fatherhood is about in these times when society is far more intrusive about defining your intimate existence. We live in world of ideologically-constructed alter-egos that come complete with a conscience – an inclination to tell you what to do and what not to do. In such a world, making one's own choices are important, and knowing the history of my father's ways and values was important to me in being able to articulate a set of values suitable for living in contemporary America.

This dialogue with my father cuts sometimes to the practical issues of finances, of how to discipline children, of where one lives or how one conducts a marriage and how all these work in a different time and place. My father is very much a part of the way that I understand my spirituality and how I confront the spiritual issues that are important in this society.

His Marxism and my Christianity become antagonists in this imagined dialogue, particularly when the place within which and about which this dialogue is taking place is America.

London was its typical self. Wet. It was Autumn 1997 and Colin Channer and I were lugging my bags through the clotted Underground; he was heading for Oxford Circle to buy some gifts for his New York family, I was making my way to Sudbury Hill on the Piccadilly line to a nicely comfortable cottage in Harrow where my Indian friend and poet, Sudeep Sen lived. On the tube, Colin talked about football. Jamaica had drawn with the USA and it seemed likely that we could make it to the World Cup Finals in France: two matches, three points needed to be one of the three. The opponents: Mexico and El Salvador. This was promising. Colin's permanent squint focused on me.

"So you never try football?"

"Yeah, lickle bit. Tried, but I wasn't good."

"Yeah? Wasn't good."

"But I used to play, kick a lickle ball here and there."

"But you play cricket."

"Yeah, man."

"So from when you start cricket."

"My father used to play in Ghana, you know?"

"So him teach you."

"You could call it dat."

There was a long pause as he stared into the newspaper again. I looked away trying to make out a headline in someone else's paper. A girl read from a novel in front of me. A black girl. I was fascinated at how far from her eyes the book was. I would be virtually eating the book to read it. My eyes are that bad. I turned to Colin, also a cornea transplant survivor. He was eating the paper. I smiled at our connection. Then he looked up.

"I can't imagine it."

"What?"

"A father. To have a father teach you things. For real. It come in like a whole different world, to even know your father and them things."

There was no self-pitying introspection there, just Colin's typically wry wonder. I knew of his fatherlessness, the epic role of parenting his mother filled with the tragic beauty of failure and remarkable success. But for the first time he was comparing his family life to mine: his fatherlessness to the presence of my father. In the silence that followed, I contemplated this. I had not seriously thought of my situation as particularly remarkable. It is not that I was unaware of friends without fathers – there were many – but I had never attempted to imagine my father not being involved in my childhood.

I was aware of the cult of fatherhood sweeping America in those days, but it seemed to have little to do with me. I observed it from a distance, curious about its cult of role-models and the goal of restoring masculinity to the American social fabric.

My detachment may have been personal, rooted in my biography, but it was largely a political coolness. After all, the urge to fatherly responsibility was coming from fairly conservative quarters: the ranks of the Promise Keepers in the wake of the celebratory March on Washington in early October. I knew about it because the men in my church were gladly in attendance. I had heard it being promoted with unprecedented decency and fairness by the media – and with zeal and prophetic passions on WMHK, the local all-Christian radio station in Columbia. When the head of the organization, a former football coach for a college team, was interviewed on NPR, I was struck by the gentleness of the interview, the absence of irony in the interviewer. The leader seemed like a genuinely committed decent guy, not a money-hungry charlatan full of cant, but a practical fellow trying to give the best face to a movement that by its very nature was exclusionary.

Women were not allowed. The touchy question of its mandate to make men the "spiritual" heads of the family, as ordained by God, was deftly softened by euphemisms and by an effort to emphasize the "service" role of the male. The Christian call for the "first to be the last" was his tactful way of arguing his case and not the Pauline dogma about husbands "being the heads of wives". I smiled at his deftness but realized that I was being a bit indulgent because I so wanted him not to be a rabid, right-wing conservative. But the truth is that he, like those drawn to the movement, wanted to make men leaders once again. Take charge. Run things. Be the bosses. And the women? They would love men for this?

This was a conservative backlash, surely. The liberation of women had become a liberation of men from the tyranny of our role, our need to be always in charge. Since there was enough of our long-constructed facade of patriarchy still standing, we could enjoy the sense of liberation we felt from not always having to lead, while still holding onto the privileges of leadership. We no longer had to take the initiative in getting involved with a woman – asking for a date or initiating the courtship ritual – but we still got to hold legal authority in marriage and social authority in the dynamics of male/female relationships. These men were out to wreck a good situation! They were out to make "men" again. And some, particularly feminists, feared they were out to undermine whatever sensitivity and commitment to equality we had acquired in the last thirty years.

There was more. The Promise Keepers were asking men to take back what was rightfully theirs: that which they had somehow relinquished to women. It would, they argued, restore the equilibrium of male/female power, something that had now gone completely haywire. Women would love men for it, they said. Somehow I was not so sure. I was not convinced that the new woman hated to lead, that she resented having become a co-partner in the firm, of sharing the burden of responsibility, the ultimate responsibility that had now moved from him to her or at least to both of them. I suspected that women saw some attraction in this new arrangement.

Indeed, the few million men who must have stumbled across (as I did) an item in the *Prime Time* television news magazine, about the triumphant joys of divorced women, must have been strangely unnerved by what we saw. Lorna, who was watching the show with me, made it clear that this was one show it was best we did not discuss afterwards. I had laughed ignorantly at the premise of the show: "Divorced women are happier than they were in the marriage, and certainly happier than the men they divorced". Her scoffing laugh was the same as she gives when she hears of some new scientific health results, such as that after $50 million dollars of intensive testing and research, it was proven that ice cream was fattening. We would laugh together at such moments. "Yeah, so they had to do a test for that! I wish someone would give me some money to do those scientific projects." Yes, I could join her then. But not this time. For the first time in years, a TV news magazine was telling me something I did not know.

The divorced women were elated. The men were a mess. Divorced men, "statistics said", died younger, much younger than divorced women. They suffered. The women were the ones who almost always asked for the divorce. The men rarely expected it. Miserable marriages were generally quite comfortable for men. Oblivious to the pain of their wives, men enjoyed all the privileges: meals, a little companionship, laundry done – all the stable things. And men did not have intimate friends to support them. While a woman would declare another woman as her best friend, a man often stumbled around helpless and alone.

So I am watching this and annoying myself by trying to match up, scared stiff to ask my wife for help. Is she miserable? Would divorce be a relief to her? Would I be a complete wreck? It was all rather silly, of course, because I ended up feeling quite secure and assured for no good reason. I did know that they were right about one thing: I liked being married. Since I got married seven years before, I had never wanted not to be married, never regretted it, despite the anxiety leading up to the marriage. I was always quite relieved and perversely proud of this fact. Perverse, because it grew out of the fear I'd had before our wedding that I would not survive the marriage, that I might fail and want to get out. I should have known better.

My assumption was that all desires and temptations, and anxieties about remaining engaged in the marriage, would stand in direct opposition to being married. The equation would go like this: want to cheat equals hate marriage, want a divorce; tired of wife equals hate marriage, want a divorce; want to live a single life again equals hate marriage etc.. Apples and oranges. The pleasures of marriage are always desirable. Men don't cheat to express their dissatisfaction with marriage as an institution. It requires a leap of the imagination for many men to connect cheating with the condition of marriage. Sex may be a problem, but we still want our domestic comforts, still want to be cherished, still want the nuclear unit – not for appearances' sake but because we genuinely want this, we like this, we need it. So when the woman says she is leaving, we are startled. For her, the equation is quite different. It does not work that way.

I was learning all this while watching the program and it dawned on me that these women pursued their freedom because they wanted power, they wanted autonomy, they wanted to be in charge. Women, like men, like this power. It makes sense. And the Promise Keepers were concluding that women did not like this power. What if women said, "No, we like the trends. Actually, we are hoping that you fellas will now work on altering the laws to give us real power, and then work on the social conventions next. Then we will be really happy!" Would the Promise Keepers say, "Okay..."? No. They would turn "in love" to Paul and say, "Hey, it is written and I did not write it. Paul did and he is God's voice."

Yet in all of this ruminating around the question of fatherhood and manhood, I did not personalize it. The Million Man March of black males was also big on the fatherhood thing; not surprisingly because the same theology of patriarchy is shared at some level by both groups. Both groups are bothered by the "emasculation" of men by feminists. I felt ideologically distant from them, and yet I shared the general spirit that called on men to be there for their families – to be fathers. Good sentiments, but sentiments not unlike the apocalyptic no smoking warnings abroad in society. Good, but I don't smoke, never did, never been tempted to except at age eleven when I decided to taste my father's cigars – his Havanas. It was funny, painful, and hardly appealing. Good message, but not really about me.

But my distance from this wave of masculinity and fatherhood may have had deeper, less obvious roots. It occurred to me that perhaps fatherhood was something I had taken for granted, something that perhaps I did not really understand because it happened around me and never drew too much attention to itself. This made the call for fathers to be always good at their duties a strange one, because I was not sure what these duties were – not in the way I know what literary terms are, what they mean and how to use them. I never acknowledged that my father was a present father. In fact, I had never regarded my father as a particularly gifted father. But then, I never imagined any other father: Neville was quite simply my father. I had problems, sometimes, with the man Neville Dawes, but as a father, he was what I had and it seemed he was adequate. Perhaps once or twice in my teen years I did compare him with other fathers. Fathers like my friend David Robertson's father, a man who used to run long distance races, make jokes about his son and about life, and whose amiable manner and casual disregard for the proprieties of adult/child distinctions made him somewhat different from my father, who rarely bantered with my friends and who seemed not so much a stickler for defining and protecting the generation "gap" but a man who just did not find it interesting. This, I have learned since, was a misapprehension. He was shy and uncertain, and his intimidating, Buddha-like glare was genetically predestined. I also learned later that many of his friends from earlier times found him most jovial and approachable. For us, Neville was not a friend; he was our father. Yet I could not say I was afraid of him. He *was* approachable. But we did not approach unless we were sure we would not be wasting his time. That is, of course, unless he had been drinking. Then he would be remarkably approachable: the best time, we quickly discovered, to get permission to go to a party or some extracurricular activity. Above all, he was a father; he was there.

He held in his head a narrative of good things for us – not so much expectations that could exert a tyranny of anxiety and fear of failure, but the dream of us in exciting places, doing exciting things, being further away from the now, and being happier for it. I know now how much care he took to stay abreast of what we were doing, what was happening around us, what we were thinking about. He was there. Always there. We could rely on this. He was going nowhere. I never feared divorce even though I knew that my father had already divorced once. The illusion of security, of a life without the rupture of divorce, was one that had held me all my childhood. I had a good father.

And his fatherhood was not entirely defined by anything he did with us. It had a great deal to do with how he was outside our home. "Your father is Neville Dawes?" This happened a lot because in Jamaica he was a public figure, a nationally known figure. To be Neville's child meant you belonged to someone and were recognized as someone of some potential. I did not really appreciate or even care for this then. But the fact of my father's status must have bolstered my self-esteem, my self-confidence, at least in the years before I began to see myself as a younger version of him and hence as a competitor – a challenger.

Then I had the feeling that my father's achievements were totally beyond me. I played cricket, but he captained the Jamaica College Team and he was a blue at Oxford. He was good. People told me this. I was okay. But I did not look anything like the fit young man that he must have been. I was good at school, but no genius. He was. I got good grades but tended to dismiss courses that I felt I would not be good at. I got competent grades at 'O' levels and won a few prizes, but I could tell that it did not compare. I consciously tried to avoid his path. I understood the pressure of a successful father and I was determined to make my own way.

In retrospect, this may explain his reluctance to give us advice. He rarely pushed and only told the stories of his exploits when he was asked. It was the modesty of a man fully aware of the way his shadow could fall on his own children. I'm sure my children won't have much to overcome to slip out from my shadow, but I am acutely aware that it is possible to put pressures on your children without meaning to do so, for I suspect that it was from that time of comparison that I became so completely aware of my inadequacies and have subsequently struggled with my own self-doubts in everything I have done. I understand too well the skill of being satisfied with mediocrity and it is what I most fear. Foggy Burrows, a soccer and athletics coach at Jamaica College, who was excellent at cajoling and doling out advice to boys who played other sports, was the first to note that quality in me. What he did not understand was that it emerged as both an appreciation of the true brilliance of others, and a manner of protecting myself from the disappointment of failure. I live with the constant anxiety that it will be revealed that I am, above everything else, mediocre.

Sometimes people read my dismissal of their praise as false modesty. It isn't. There are intense periods when I honestly doubt the value of my work.

And yet, even as I write the above, I know there is a falsehood at work there too. After all, despite my suspicions, I know that I remain driven by the desire to do the things I do well. I also know that to deny the fact that I have written very good works would be to suffer from an abject case of false modesty. There is a contradiction in all this. I am hard on myself, knowing how much better the work can be; and yet I know that the work has value, has merit. I think of my father's unwritten novel and see much of him in this.

In America, there are standard expectations placed on the so-called ideal Dad. I had not read these anywhere but I have absorbed them through some kind of osmosis. They are: Dad should have a job; Dad should be handy and teach handiness; Dad should teach a child a sport – especially a boy child; Dad should take boys to games; Dad "should be there" for the child. The image I have of this Dad is more vivid than the list would suggest. This is the Dad Model I observed when I had to join my son's preschool class on a visit to the State Zoo. I could tell that I was doing a very "Dad" thing and that the other Dads there (there were as many as four, along with two or three mums and two teachers) were quite proud of their Daddy deeds. They were, as men, quite self-conscious about the uniqueness of this moment, of their gesture. This was a task normally undertaken by women. One man, a tall black man, who struck me as rather mature to have children so young, was beaming. He explained it clearly to me in an educated Northern black accent, polished by an extraordinary cheer and brightness.

"It is fantastic that so many men are doing this," he said. "Yeah, usually women do this kind of thing. I have been at some of these things and..." he moved his mouth but made no sound, as if attempting a conspiracy to protect the women from being offended. I had already tagged him as a Promise Keeper man: unwilling to offend the poor women, but clear about his place. He continued softly, "...I mean no men, just these women. So this is good because Dads ought to be Dads. We need that now."

Perhaps I was seduced by the sense of self-importance in doing the right thing as a father that he so smugly emanated. That I should be drawn to the wholesome scent of righteousness was predictable.

It is a part of my make-up, a defect, really, that deprives me of much that a more hard-boiled, pragmatic attitude would give me access to: like the way I approached what was clearly a cut-throat dialogue about who of the fifteen regular players on my university cricket team would get to tour the West Indies for the biannual Campus Games. I wanted to go. I deserved to go. I was one of the best batsmen in the team and I always played and played well. We sat in the shade of the dusty pavilion at the end of an afternoon of practice to discuss the team. Goats and stray children from the community across the fence loitered around, as if waiting for someone to suggest a game or some diversion. I assumed much: that I was a shoo-in, that we would do the right thing and pick the best team, that good sense would prevail. So I observed with some detachment the pathetic display of useless players making what I thought were hopeless claims for their inclusion. Gradually, the talk degenerated into insult and abuse; people were dredging up game after game and the way certain people had lost their wicket or given up precious runs. The loudest voices were those of the least talented. Good sense would prevail. I decided to do the right thing and exercise a bit of reverse psychology to impress upon them the ludicrous nature of their claims.

"Look, I can't take this foolishness, man." I said. "So what,

you can't look at the scores and know what the best team is?"
I was cowed down: stats are not everything, chemistry, consistency,
no country experience, and so on. And for a fleeting moment,
but one long enough for me to wreck it all, I lost my cool. I
played the final reverse psychology card.

"Okay, if you people can honestly say that I don't deserve
to travel with the team, then cut me. I would like to go, but if
you can't be fair or pick the best team and if some of you are
so desperate to want to go at the expense of the team's success,
then drop me. I will live." I waited only a few seconds before
one of the thugs spoke.

"Okay, Dawes don't want to go. Let's see who we have now."
I waited for protest, I looked around me. There was no support;
in fact, there was some relief in their eyes. I was dropped. I
realized then that the world was simply not going to succumb
to the pressures of good sense and fairness.

Despite these lessons, I am still drawn into the seduction of
good sense. I started to feel good about myself as a father at the
zoo. I wondered if people were noticing me. I indulged in some
pride, I admit, seduced by the storybook world of brilliant sunshine
darting in sudden spurts through the canopy of trees and shrubbery,
the animals, the serenity of it all. With my son, taking a day off
work to be a father – it was all so right. The Promise Keeper
Dad saw a ready convert and he stuck close, feeding me with
self-congratulatory notes about ourselves. I struggled to reassure
myself of my integrity, because I recognized it was all a sham –
even while I indulged. I shook off the man – thankfully before
he started to appeal to our mutual blackness and our uniqueness
as black men who were into fatherhood and marriage in a manner
that ran counter to "our people's" pattern. I did not want to
hear this at all.

Despite my well-cultivated sense of irony, I was feeling bad
that this was my first such outing ever. I was one of those men,
those not-so-good men, reneging on his role as a father. I was

almost tempted to explain about my job and writing, but just rescued myself from embarrassment in time. I nodded. He knew fatherhood, understood the language, wore the purple school tee shirt and talked to kids with the pitch and diction of a practised television talker-to-kid person. He was a Mr. Rogers in black face – a Sesame Street Dad-type. I was neither of these. I wanted to get out of the zoo. I grew tired of these children easily and had a habit of talking to them "normally". This was not fun for the children, but they listened to me when I spoke. I was left wanting in the good father stakes. It turned out that my zoo companion *was* a Promise Keeper and a good one, too.

I did not, nor do I fit that kind of stereotyped model, and my father, I always felt, did not fit it either. But my father was a better father than I gave him credit for, because my father changed – he was a real person who changed with us. I did not really understand this until I started to chart the various stages of his relationship with us. The father I had was ubiquitous enough when we were children; in this alone, I was immensely different from Colin Channer. So my father was there: we have quite specific memories of him as a part of our lives. He was the souse-maker each Christmas in Ghana, but he was also the vicious defender of the sacredness of his study in those days; it was of him that we chanted when one of us had committed some heinous crime and the time of his return home was upon us: "Neville is coming! Neville is coming!" He was there buying us precious hamburgers at the Senior Common Room while he drank and shouted with his cronies. He would pile us into the car, take us up the hill, supply us with roasted nuts, burgers, and sodas and then leave us to entertain ourselves in the yard of broad-canopied trees while he held court inside. But we had quality time with my father: he was there. He was there to declare to us on special evenings: "I am going to dine", but we thought he was saying "die", and for a long time we worried for him as he left the house decked in funeral black and his cap and gown. He was there. He was there to take us to the polo field in Achimota to watch him play cricket. He was there to order my older brother to strip naked and take a bucketful of water to kill a bush fire he had lit in our backyard; he was there to rescue me from the maiming of my hair when my mother was away and the helper had impetuously taken chunks from my head. Neville took me onto the verandah after he got home and trimmed my bawling self to a barbered evenness. He was there to play monopoly with us. He was there, and in this I had something quite stable and distinctive, I suppose.

My father did not, as far as I can recall, ever say, "I love you" to me when I was a child. This was no cliché of tough manhood. I suspect that he saw affection as action, a gathering of all of us to tell jokes, a plethora of fascinating gifts, always specific to each one of us, and a genuine interest in our lives. But he used to write to us faithfully when he was away on his visits abroad. It was in those letters that we came to expect his expressions of love. "I love you, Kwame..." In later years he would say it, say that he loved his children, but we had no doubt that he did because he had written those words on the pale blue air-letters that arrived at our home from Russia, China, North Africa, Oxford, London, Las Palmas – from all over the world.

But it was his expressions of endearment for my mother that most assured us. They were not all over each other in their affections, but in his letters home, the words "Chochoo, I love you and miss you a lot" seemed so scandalously sentimental that we would all smile at it – but were reassured by the words. We needed to know that my father loved my mother; we needed to know that my mother loved my father – loved each other enough to say those words. We could hear her saying, "We love you, Neville," on the phone. It was her coded phrase of endearment, of intimacy. But sometimes she would say the words "I love you, Neville," and we warmed at the security of that.

For there were times when it was possible to feel that love was threatened. They fought – argued loudly and painfully. There was the startling night when I was in my late teens when my mother seemed to have decided that we were now old enough to know that they had sex and that physical contact between them meant something. After a week of disquieting silence, of a powerfully volatile stalemate, my mother finally spoke. She said she could not stand his silence any more, his punishment. We wanted her to stop, wanted her to keep us in the dark about her pain, about his neglect, but she would not cater to our fear of embarrassment.

"Neville," she said. "You have not even touched me in weeks."

He said nothing. He looked at her. It was almost too painful to watch his inability to respond, to find a way out of his predicament. We all looked away, pretending that we did not understand what was being said. Like most arguments between them, this one, too, faded. But I kept a record of it. I made another vow to always be there, to always touch, to express love to my wife in ways that could reassure my children, in ways I had wanted to be reassured.

I came to realize that my anxieties about marriage came out of my fear that I would be a husband like my father was. I felt, when faced with the prospect of marrying Lorna, that what I had to offer, was, I suspected, much like Neville had offered, not the stuff of good husbandry.

The truth is that during those years I did not know a great deal about the insides of my parents' marriage. Part of the problem, I have come to realize, is that I did not know anything about marriage, about what allows two people to remain together, committed and steadfast for almost thirty years. I know better now that my father was a good husband in the flawed way that many man are.

But faced with the prospect of my own marriage, I feared those things that infuriated me about my father: his stoic silence, his unswerving commitment to an ideology that might not hold up in the face of change; and by the awareness that somehow and for some reason, a man, a husband, could really hurt his wife. I feared those things in me.

This litany is not one I would ever have offered as a model of good fatherhood because I never really regarded it as a model. Indeed, there was a period during the 1980s when I started to recognize some of my father's traits in me. I worried about them. For the first time I felt a helpless feeling of predestination, of being part of a forgone fate. I did not want to be like him. I was enacting the ritual of fathers and sons. It is not that I disliked him, but I did not ever want to use silence as a deadly weapon to punish the people I loved. My father was a remarkable wielder of silence and my mother was often on the receiving end of it. When I found myself doing the same thing with a girlfriend, I worried. It came so naturally to me and it was so viciously effective. I prayed and prayed that I would be able to fight it. I then developed one of my many comfort theories: theories designed for a life of calm and reassurance. I concluded that while many of my father's traits seemed to want to reside in me, I would make sure that they would not dominate me. I would fight them, fight them. I would talk more to my children, discuss everything with my wife, and I would never allow the silent treatment to emerge as a weapon.

But my father was quite clearly a good father. Unfortunately, he died before I could consolidate his legacy, before I could extricate myself from his shadow, and before I could become his friend and find access to his past – the world that for long remained unavailable to me.

Recently, I was given a pile of letters he had written over a thirty year period beginning in 1957 when he was about thirty-years old. I was discovering a fascinating man. I wrote of his

143

passing some years after his death, calling him: "O world that I have lost." I could finally begin to grasp the meaning of being fatherless. I sought fathers in others. Not to replace Neville, but to pick up where he had left off. Neville died before he could nurture me as a protégé, as a fellow artist. Perhaps there would be none of my intense need to have my work affirmed by senior artists had he been able to see my writing and offer judgment on it. I have imagined what it would be like today were I able to show him my collections of poetry and sit down to discuss the work. Would he look at my manuscripts, offer suggestions? He did for others. O world that I have lost. I replaced him with people like John Ruganda, a Ugandan playwright whom I studied with in New Brunswick, Canada. It was a quest for guidance, stability and affirmation. But it is impossible to fill the gap with someone else. Impossible. And equally daunting, if not more so, when there was no father in the first place.

Colin and I had reached a curious impasse: I had no language with which to speak of having a father and he could barely articulate the meaning of such an absence in his life. What we shared was the fact that we were now fathers seeking to be good fathers because of and inspite of the past.

In the end, I came to understand that regardless of how much I missed in my relationship with Neville, I can be sure of one thing: I was fathered. He wrote about me in his letters, talked about his hopes for me. All of this I discovered when I read these letters years after his death. They have been a deep, abiding comfort.

So even though I took his fathering for granted, I can't do so now. The truth is he took his fathering seriously. He knew how to be entertained by his children and he knew these children well. He left us little in terms of material wealth, but he left his presence, his engagement and his sense of responsibility and hope in us.

CHAPTER 9

...where the heart is...?
on being at home in america

My children will not have to contend with any thin gene-thread of inherited Marxism. What they may well pick up, however, are its ghostly symptoms – a condition that I recognize creeping into my language, my thoughts and my actions every so often. My vestigial Marxism was never grounded in a landscape. I had no romantic notions of Russia or China. Cuba is a favourite place of mine because I have always liked the underdog and I have come to respect tremendously the difference that socialism has made to many of the people of that country. But Cuba is mostly glorious to me as part of my memory of the ideological headiness of Jamaica in the seventies. Cuba is part of my myth of identity, but it is not as if I regularly get into full blown arguments with Americans about Cuba or plan to abscond there to live out the rest of my days. My intellectual Marxism is wanting. I did read some of the texts and I understand what Marx meant by the class struggle, but I always found the whole business far less self-defining than the Bible, even if my reading of the Bible is heavily shaped by egalitarian ideas. But my children will not hear me declare myself a Marxist, nor am I likely to teach them the 'Internationale' as my father did us.

Despite this, my children will see Marxist shadings in my

attitudes. But they couldn't be blamed for not labelling them as such. The truth is, I am bastardizing the word Marxism when I use it this way. What they will see, then, is ambivalence.

They will see someone who always questions the validity of the American world role. They will see me arguing with the television and groaning at the forcible interventions of the American government in other countries. But these symptoms probably have far less to do with a thin thread of Marxism and more to do with a well-cultivated anti-American instinct that is a disguised form of nationalism. For instance, they will observe my unwillingness to celebrate Thanksgiving and quite quickly grasp the problems of genocide that this holiday conjures up for me. They may hear me try to argue that cricket and football (read soccer) are superior to every American game, even if I watch the NBA games religiously and sneak a look at the NFL games when I can. They will hear me constantly refer to "home" as somewhere other than America. They will note that we prefer the term Native Americans to Indians. Indeed, the children early busied themselves correcting their teachers at school on this issue. We were amused by the inferences probably drawn from this peculiarity in their parents. Yes, they learnt that "graduating" from kindergarten was not a milestone as far as we were concerned, and that getting a university degree is a fairly basic qualification for life. These are not strange expectations or quirks, but I can hear them talking about their weird parents with their friends. But all of these are superficial signs of cultural preference. They will not help them to come to a sense of who they are, and what nationality they can claim as their own.

I knew that my children would find themselves searching for an answer to the question of what it means to call a place home, because, after only six years of living in America, I had begun to sense my inclination towards calling South Carolina "home". True, the inclination withered under scrutiny – or at least scored low on the questionnaire I then used to test my loyalty to the cause of not being seduced by the myth of a new home: (1) Are other sports – American sports – becoming more important to me than cricket? This is, in truth, a strange and complicated question, not because it is hard to answer, but because of what is embedded in the question. After all, why cricket? What is so important about this colonial British game to me? Why should I value cricket over American sports? Is it merely a kind of Anglophile neurosis? But then, cricket is not an English game in my mind, just as English is not a British language to me. Cricket is wholly West Indian. It is a game that I played as a child, a game that has obsessed me, a game that I first saw in Ghana, the game my father played and his father before him and so on. If I stop loving cricket, I can forget about finding home in the Caribbean or even in Ghana. (2) Do I cheer American teams when they are playing against non-European teams? This is simple: my sense of home is ideologically situated in the Third World. To cheer America would mean that I had bought into the inordinate patriotism of Americans that makes them fly flags outside their homes as if otherwise passers-by might mistake them for foreigners – or worse, might forget exactly what country this is. (3) Have I begun to understand the allure of cheerleading? No. But I do like the US basketball team to win and do so handily. And I secretly enjoy American domination in boxing. (4) Am I comfortable with the idea of being buried in the earth of America? (5) Have I begun to wonder how people who don't live in America manage, how they survive? (6) Do I feel as if I really belong in the line when I arrive at customs and join the US Citizens line? (7) Have I overcome the feeling that at some point the immigration people are going to write me a letter giving me two days to leave the country?

I generally did well at that test. But there were moments when I forgot myself. Then, I panicked, because if I could forget myself, then what of these children of ours who had no reference points, no cricket, no other landscape, no memories of another time to counter their sense of America as home? And I wondered whether it was fair of me to want to prevent them from embracing America.

In 1998, on a trip to the UK, all these ideas took on a striking significance. I was in London and I was thinking seriously about what became this book. I was on a reading tour to promote some new poetry I had published in Britain. I realized I was abroad, away from "home" when I found myself depending on the long distance calls to South Carolina for my sense of stability. I made most of the calls from a call box on Greenford Road, a few hundred yards from where I was staying. My friends would have allowed me to use their phone, but I wanted to call without feeling guilty about racking up phone bills. I would collect coins all day preparing for that late night phone call. It would be late afternoon in Columbia. The children would be waiting around for dinner. I could see the quality of light in the white and wood-brown dining area, the familiar tiles, the sense of home, I suppose.

The connection carried the voices clean, as if they were next door, despite the thousand odd miles of sea. I chewed on soggy chips, while counting out every bit of spare change with grease and vinegar-slippery fingers. Outside was the rain, the cold, the darting yellows, reds, greens, and oranges of the traffic, the clouds of bodies under umbrellas floating past; the glass of the phone booth pimpled with raindrops which broke up the view outside, making it all surreal: another place, another life.

I just wanted to hear their voices, to remind myself of myself. I am a writer, yes, and there are times when I do feel caught up in that, as if I am someone else, as if there is a part of me that is defined and explained entirely by that. It happens especially when I travel; people ask questions expecting compact, digestible answers: I live in South Carolina; I was born in Ghana but grew up in Jamaica; I teach; I write – poems, yes. Everything is predicated on why I am here. I am here to read my poems, to make some money, to lecture. I am a writer.

That night I had been seduced by the bright applause of an overflowing audience in the Poetry Café tucked under the Poetry Society's offices. A jazz combo had played, and then an open-mike period gave other poets a chance to read. I remember a woman in black with a scrubbed face that looked extraordinarily white because of the strands of black hair falling over her eyes. She read poems about being a divorced mother with an ex in an American jail and of being threatened with deportation for taking her daughter out of the country without his consent. I remember the introductions to her poems better than the poems themselves. America had made her so militant, so defiant. She was proud of this. Her poems did not shine like her story, like her face. But I liked her, the poetry of her. She made me feel I was a writer, a poet somehow shaped by the moment.

I read and sang, my voice playing games with the rhythms stitched into my lines. Sometimes you "zone", you soar at a reading. A giddy bravado takes over and you literally sing. You begin to believe in the myths you have written, you believe in your poetry. After the reading, one of the organizers, a man of intense eyes and a head as enigmatic and forceful as a grainy photograph of a street-walking maverick in some wintry Eastern European cityscape pulled me aside. I listened to him, drawn into his dream of me. I wanted witnesses. I felt like Macbeth before the witches on the heath. He spoke in soft tones.

"When I was living in Chicago, years ago, I used to run a reading series. We had T.S. Eliot, W.H. Auden, Pound, Dylan Thomas, Gunn, you name them." There was no boasting in his tone – always flat, even, calm. He was making a greater point. I tried to calculate his age: he was up there; he must have been to know these men, these great poets.

"I heard all of them. I will tell you this; of all of them the only one to match you as a reader was Dylan Thomas." I was buying the whole thing. I wanted to buy it, I suppose. The difficulty of accepting all this from a guy I hardly knew just faded away. I was giddy from the applause and I liked what I heard. It did not matter how unlikely it was for someone to have heard all these people at some point in his life. I did not do the math. I did not *want* to do the math. This supernatural soliciting... I was a father who lived in a house in the suburbs of Columbia with a telephone bill unpaid, and a bank account so thoroughly overdrawn it was frightening. I only wore good shoes whenI had to. People knew when I had a new shirt. The maverick manner of my attire was no longer a matter of choice – this was all I had. I had three children who made me wonder what I was passing on to them. This supernatural soliciting...

He was smiling now. I was testing his credibility. This is almost impossible to do in England. In America, people find ways to announce themselves, to establish their credentials quickly and efficiently. In England there is a cultish belief in the enactment of the biblical idiom, "Be kind to all, for you may be entertaining angels in your midst." Almost to a fault, the English understate their worth. The less ostentatious, the more likely their pedigree is lofty. I could not read this man. He was part of a clutch of art types linked to the Poetry Society. He had always been generous about my work. Tonight, he was confessing. He was sincere. I knew this much, for after I read the long poem "Progeny of Air" to end my reading, he came to the mike to thank me, his throat gurgling with phlegm, his eyes watering. I was nonplussed. I had no words. I wanted to vanish back to the familiar slackness of my life, the idle watching of television with Lorna lying on the sofa dozing and the children coughing through the monitor – the comforts of our truth. I wanted to be in the brightly-lit basement church of our Baptist fellowship of charismatic believers, longing for that great revival. I wanted to be that helplessly hopeful man straining to touch that flame of spirit in this contained world of belief, with a longing to find a lightness of being, a cleanness of soul there in the heart of America's South, with all its contradictions, its most unpoetic realities. There, being a poet means little. Even at the University, I was among colleagues who did not read my books, did not find anything remarkable in a published poet. I did not have the imprint. I was quite normal. And in a strange way, I had found comfort in that. But here, this man, with his sparsely-haired head, leaned into my face and spoke mysteries.

"Let's make a wager. It is a friendly wager, a few pounds, no more, but I would pay up if I am wrong. I don't know how long it will take, but I have heard you, read you, I have seen all of them and I will make you a wager..." He waited for me to nod. I could tell that he was uncomfortable with this profusion, with his enthusiasm, with his confession. Before he continued, he apologized as if he could sense my discomfort, my unwillingness to be pulled into a strange belief. "Really, I am sorry about doing this. I don't mean to waste your time, to embarrass you or me."

"It's okay. It's okay." I said, not convinced. I waited. He held his hand out.

"You will win the Nobel Prize soon." He said it quickly. It was now like a curse – a strange portent that quickened me and that I wanted to reject because he was sincere. He sounded as if he had been told this by someone important. I laughed too loudly, trying to spit out the idea, to drive it away. To believe this was to be drawn into madness. He grabbed my hand, squeezed it. "A friendly wager." Then he let go, looked shyly away and hurried away to organize things.

I wanted to be with Lorna, immediately. She was the only one I could confess this to. To relate this to anyone else would be to brag, to suggest a strange acceptance of the portent. I did not believe it, and still don't, but just repeating it amounted to an admission of the thought. But his words had warmed me. I was assured of good things, perhaps. And the crass hustler in me enjoyed the thought that this good man, this pure lover of verse, was a supporter, someone who maybe could help. He offered to do anything, anything he could for me. I loved the prospect. Still, I wanted to tell someone. Lorna would understand, she would laugh at it, laugh with the gentlest faith in me. She would be as ironic as I would want to be: distant, yet warmed.

I closed into myself on the long train ride on the Piccadilly line to Sudbury Hill. The lull, the aloneness, the constant noise of the train put me back in South Carolina, back into the details of my life there, and the glory of the moment became a dwindling sensation. My mind was on my father again and his inability to be other than a writer, to be other than a man who mastered silence, mastered the art of seeming distant, lost in his own world. These last, perhaps, had something to do with a prophecy unfulfilled – a promise of greatness – the great Ghana/Jamaica novel he never wrote. But in those silent moments, when he seemed so far away, clouded by the blue smoke of his cigarettes, he seemed like a stranger, not a father, seemed like a thinker, a creature caught up with the myth of his identity. I imagined he was contemplating deep ideas, constructing concepts too important, too significant to be ignored or interrupted by the simple mundaneness of fatherhood. I would watch him totally cloud out all of us, my mother especially, and I would resent it. I vowed never to be like that. I vowed never to be caught up in a dream of greatness.

So, on the train, I could sense the danger of falling into this. I wanted to talk to Lorna. She would pull me back into the familiar. She would remind me of the simplicity of fathering, the poem of living with children, the fact of our debts and our way of coping, constantly loving, laughing, being there to talk, to listen, to be in it together.

It was raining steadily at Sudbury Hill station; puddles of

light from the street lamps flowed over the dented asphalt platform. Everyone moved slowly. It was the last train, and the weary plodded home, blankly, as if completely taken over by the monotony of their lives. We all carried secrets, our ways of smiling inside, but we held them close. In London, you become so alert to the strangeness of people's secrets because they wear nothing on their sleeves. Perversions seem startling, for there is a veneer of moral order that people wear: it is in the blank face, the depthless gaze, the unreadable silence.

I told Lorna everything. She laughed and asked how much money the prize would be worth. We laughed and talked about the children, gossiped about friends, counted the days. I wanted to be with her. It was cold. The coins were vanishing too quickly and outside the cold seemed threatening.

I walked home contemplating the great poem I would write. It did not come. The man's words were seeping out of me. It was as if the spitting rain was washing it from my body. Everything was being disturbed by the rain. I pulled my hood over my face and limped through the puddles, longing for the simplicity of South Carolina and my total insignificance there. I think I understood something of my father's mind in those moments. Something about the things he used to do when he was away. As children, we imagined that he relished his times abroad, away from us, that he enjoyed the strange lands where he met great people and drank good liquor all night, forgetting us, not quite missing us.

Lorna had been in England and I in Canada when I began to make my case to her. It was an old case, one she had heard before in Jamaica when I suggested that we get back together after a four-year hiatus. I spent my time comparing myself to other men – real men, I thought. These men could drive cars, fix cars, fix houses, do lawns, handle tools, make things with their hands. These men would have good jobs, build a home for the family, love their children, be there to play football with the boys, farm, hustle any amount of money, invest – a whole barrage of things I suspected I had no talent for. I told her that I would not represent stability; that I was a writer who might well become a teacher. I saw no wealth in my future. My father had left no inheritance, no home, not even the example of how to buy a home. I was not a good prospect. I was blabbering on in this way when she interrupted me.

"It is the very things you say you are that make me love you. I am not in love with traits. I am in love with you." Today, it sounds quite romantic, but at the time, it seemed like a most pragmatic and reasonable articulation. I accepted love. She travelled to Canada, into a sturdy winter, and we got married after the thaw in a small chapel on the hills of the University of New Brunswick campus. An old, almost dotish, but entirely sweet man performed the ceremony while our new friends, from a world away from what we called home, came to pay tribute. It was not the kind of grand wedding expected of Kwame and Lorna – that Jamaican wedding in the large university chapel in Mona with singers from all the groups we had worked with and family, family, family. We were both travellers who had managed to learn the skills of making home in a strange climate and this wedding was an affirmation of the singular love we were embarking on. It was romantic, but weddings ought to be that. Still, it showed us something of how our lives might progress in the years ahead. It established the simple improvisation of learning everything for ourselves, of relying on our own experiences and our private history to sustain us. We were not being groomed into any one else's ritual of marriage, no one was planning the details, no one was whispering traditions into our ears – we were making our world and something important was happening.

My mother travelled to New Brunswick to be there. The timing of the wedding made it impossible for Lorna's parents to make it. About four friends from Jamaica came. They were all living in America at the time, so it was possible for them to make it across the border. Beyond that, Jamaica was far away. We felt a strange sense of freedom and control because of this. Perhaps it was what we had always longed for, as Lorna and I were never especially successful at conforming to the expectations of those around us in Jamaica. There, our friendship was always strained by the presence of friends, of family, and the business of social expectation. But away from it all, forging our own rules, our own principles of relating, we were steady, constant, and exceptionally honest.

By the time Sena was born two years later, it was clear that we were learning the twisted pleasures and pain of being immigrants, being away from home. So that moment in the phone booth, talking to Lorna, was shaped by all the years of being a pair, of having to make up our own language, our own manner of reading each other. Being travellers gave us space to dream, to laugh at each other, to depend fully on each other.

Perhaps it was the same sense of escape from the conformist pressures of Jamaican middle-class society that attracted my father to Ghana, that led him to feel that his most pleasant years were lived far from Jamaica, in an alien world that was only temporarily his home. In Ghana, he had the chance to reinvent himself, to become the politically daring Marxist who would bring excitement and adventure to our home, and the artist who would gather around him younger poets, playwrights, and pioneering spirits whom he would impress with his wit, his broad knowledge. These were people who were attracted to a man who was wholly self-generated. His surname meant nothing in Ghana. It would have been different in Jamaica – he would have been defined by his father's legacy, by the status of the family. In Canada I came to understand the appeal of the Ghanaian world for him and his feeling of imprisonment in Jamaica when he returned in 1971, where he seemed to change, become more serious, less social, less the devilish figure of enjoyment and witty banter. He was cautious in Jamaica because the minefields were too familiar to him – the minefields of social expectation, the history of his first marriage, of class, of the ferocity of middle-class conservatism under its thin veneer of respectability. It was clear to us, even as children, that my father was a different man at home in Jamaica, and it would take its toll on him for the rest of his life. For him, this was a strange homecoming. He wanted to return and yet he knew that he was giving up something that was dear to him: friendship and the fresh world of self-definition that is one of the pleasures of being an immigrant.

I understood this now. In Canada, I became a reggae singer and startled everyone in Jamaica. Kwame was not a singer, not really a musician. I would never have been a reggae singer in Jamaica – I would not have been free to be that.

But there were differences. In North America, I was not as happy as my father clearly was in Ghana. I could not be. He entered a world in which there existed no tradition of being a minority West Indian black man in a largely black society. He was inventing himself, his role, his status. There, he was learning about the genius of black leadership, of Pan-Africanist idealism, a force uncomplicated by the colour nuances of the Jamaican racial fabric. In Ghana he was able to find a place of connection and belonging. I could never find such a place in America. I could only be grafted onto a tradition of racial abuse, of segregation and oppression, and the counter-tradition of survival, resistance and cultural creation, but it would be hard to invent myself in this world because the dialectics were already determined.

But there is a space in which Lorna and I have reconstructed ourselves and sought to find new selves. It has been the place where we have tried to reconcile the anxieties of our relationship, our marriage. Distant from Jamaica, we have found ways to work through old fears and old patterns. I did not want to be like my father: a silent husband torturing my wife with an inscrutable wall of muteness. I did not want to be so caught up in the myths of my writer's world that the pragmatics of life were ignored. I wanted to make some sense of our living in ways that defied the tyranny of inheritance.

I needed to talk to Lorna on the phone that night in London, because I was being seduced by the promise of greatness. I did not want to be so caught up in the myths of my writer's world that the pragmatics of life were ignored. The irony is that it was the quiet language of our mundane world, our world of being caught in the stranglehold of consumerist America, that quieted my intoxication. We rehearsed the financial situation – a massive mortgage, the result of our determination to stop renting and own; an overdue payment for a four-year-old loan taken out to pay a surprise tax bill from Canada; an overdrawn checking account that was bleeding us with the maddening twenty-five-dollar-a-check fee for anything overdrawn; the maxed credit cards: all the common language of American life. We were caught in it. It was part of the seduction of America and its debilitating force. But it was what I needed to quiet me, to draw me out of the seduction of a dream, a dream world that was almost always nipping at the edges of my father's imagination.

I know I am a poet, but it was in my discomfort with the temptations of this poet-self that a truth about "home" so struck me. Escaping from the temptation of an obsession with literary greatness, away from home, away from family, I could start to understand how this other place, this place called America, could somehow become home. In this construction, home is about comfort, about where one feels most normal, most oneself. The temptation is to reduce home to that nuclear space: I am home when I am with my wife and children. The temptation is strong because in an alien place you draw closer, you are more dependent on each other, you actually work harder to create a sense of home. But in your mind, lingering, is a sense

157

that you are reconstructing home, and that at some point soon what you build will not be enough. It creeps upon you when you least expect it, when you notice families with grands and great-grands gathering in large packs to enact the rituals of their history. You see it when you walk through graveyards and search in vain for a familiar name; you sense it when you want your children to be able to dig deeper than the shallow soil of your immediate existence to find a memory of themselves, an answer to the ubiquitous mystery of their genes. Then the home of the nuclear family is not enough; it falls short.

I walked through the icy rain warm from the talk with Lorna somehow grounded. These are the small pleasures of exile. I would return to South Carolina and find everything familiar, comfortable. Our bed, the light, the car, the garden, the shower, the television. They are superficial things, but I fear that every time I leave and return, I am letting go of my alienness, my sense of distance. I fear it, for it means I may be embracing something that will prove shallow and quite useless in the future. For I am not like those who came to escape, longing to reinvent myself entirely. I like my past; I love my roots, long to hold on to them. So how to be here and not here?

CHAPTER 10

fathering the son

The business of having children in America complicated the meaning of home. Kekeli, my son, was the first birth in America. Sena's Canadian birth was exciting because it was the first and though there were complications about nationality and identity, because we thought at the time that we would be returning to Jamaica to live, we were more thrilled by the prospect of having a child, by the miracle of her birth and by the weight of responsibility upon us. Sena, we understood, would be a Canadian-born Jamaican, and this was quite appropriate for it fitted nicely with the Dawes/Davis model of identity. As nomads, we were used to hyphens in our identities as long it was clear where the grounding was. My father, moreover, had no quarrel with Canada. Further, Sena's birth in Canada could prove handy to her later in life when college choices and that kind of thing became an issue. At least she would have a few more options than I had.

But Kekeli was different. By the time of his birth, I had a permanent job in Sumter, and the paperwork was already being processed for our green cards. We were permanent residents in America and he was about to be born in this country. Before Keli's birth we knew that we would be moving into new realms of definition of self and home. But when I knew it was a boy, another weight fell upon me. Now I had a son, an American son, a black boy living in America!

Kekeli was not just born. He was pulled out of my wife's open womb, blooded and coated in thick wetness, his fist curled, his body twisting into life, while the gruff-voiced anaesthetist hovered over Lorna. Lorna's doctor maintained her very Irish joviality through it all.

"There it is, there it is," she said as she pulled the umbilical cord that was coiled tightly around the baby's neck. "Now breathe, go on."

I realized in that moment that the baby could have died in the labour room. We had been going through the rituals of breathing, counting out contractions, and wondering about dilation. The monitors suggested a sluggish heartbeat, but nothing to worry about. I was even thinking that the books I had brought and the essays to be marked might not remain undisturbed for the rest of the night. At this pace, the child would be born, Lorna would get some sleep and I would mark the papers in the quiet of the hospital. At that point, Lorna's contractions had been climbing on top of each other and tumbling into themselves.

Then Dr. Anderson had rushed into the birthing room with the look of someone who had just gotten herself together. She came in and announced what we had already surmised: Lorna was ready to push. Lorna was now quite tired. The epidural had relaxed the muscles in her legs and she kept saying, "I can't push, I can't feel to push." Dr. Anderson, though, came around to Lorna to reassure her. I kept the ice coming.

As she began to push, it became clear from the monitors that the baby was in trouble. I looked at the faces of the nurses. They could not conceal their panic. I turned to Dr. Anderson, whose left hand rested on Lorna's stomach, while her gloved right hand felt deeply into her, her face in the kind of concentrated stare that suggested that she was feeling for something. The probing done, Dr. Anderson was firing instructions around the room. People were rushing about. I was strangely calmed by my inability to do anything. I held Lorna, I tried to will good things around us.

"Don't push, Lorna, when the next contraction comes. Just relax. We have to take you in to do an emergency C. I think the baby is in some distress. But it will be great; the thing is planning to give us a great adventure today – that thing, that thing." I looked at her for some reassurance. She smiled noncommittally. Then everything was a blur. The papers for Lorna to sign were on her lap. She was laid back and pushed out of the room. I followed the bed into the operating room while soothing Lorna, trying to keep her calm.

As Lorna slipped away under the anaesthetic, I spoke to her, rubbing her scalp and brushing back the hair from her forehead. Then I stepped back and watched the whole operation in the clear blue light. The slip of blood on the skin, the clamping, then the business of dislodging the infant. The doctor showed me the baby: he had a penis. It was a boy. I panicked; I truly panicked.

I was not prepared for a boy. I had already decided that another girl would fit in easily with what I knew. Somehow, a girl seemed more manageable. We had taken Sena home and I learnt about her, her feeding habits, her hunger, her stomach pains, her diaper rash, how she liked being bathed, how she liked to sleep, the way to carry her, the way to feel her warmth coming through my skin. Above all, I learned to connect her large, dark, inquiring eyes with my flesh, my person. This was my daughter, our daughter – a part of me. It was a novelty, but by the time Keli arrived, Sena had become a part of who we now were, part of our definition of family. We had already travelled several thousand miles with her: from Canada to Jamaica, all around Jamaica and then from there to Sumter, South Carolina. Lorna had taught me how to clean her when she stooled; details about a girl's vulnerability to vaginal infections, details that were alien to me before that. I learnt to be comfortable with the delicacy of her body, to not panic at things girls did, to accept that as father of this baby girl, I had to learn the language of being a father. I learned it all quite well, and had grown used to learning new things – something I usually don't much like.

I am a creature of habit, finding comfort in being familiar with the rituals of life. When I learn a route to work or school, I generally stick to it. When I discovered a taste for pistachio nuts, I bought bag after bag of them and ate them steadily and almost obsessively for months. Canteen workers, after three weeks, like to give me my meal before I ask for it. They smile, waiting for me to look shocked at how well they know me. Were I to experiment with drugs, I would probably become efficiently addicted. I *can* shift habits, can move to something else when I have tired of one thing, but am drawn to the familiar – always. A boy after Sena would shatter my routine and disrupt the familiar. Another girl would be easy – no learning curve.

Lorna grew; I talked to the child at night – quoting Shakespeare, playing reggae, praying softly through the protection of flesh and fluid. And meantime Sena grew. She became familiar. She ate what was given, slept when we expected her to. Her character was taking shape. It seemed as if we had worked hard to get to where we were with her. I liked the familiarity, I did.

So when Dr. Anderson turned Kekeli and a penis came in to view, I saw the worm of his gender and right then, my stomach unfurled. A son! At that moment, I realized that familiarity had been taken away. We had a son and immediately the considerations changed. Was he to be circumcised? We had agreed he would be. We had read about circumcision and decided to go with a family tradition and have him circumcised. It was my first decision as the father of a son and I realized how difficult my responsibilities as father would be. With Sena, I turned to

Lorna for knowledge about female anatomy, the way it works. I understood that I relied on Lorna to teach me what needed to be done with Sena, because I assumed that their gender connection made her best qualified.

The birth of a boy wrenched me away from that comfortable dependency. I was the one with the penis, I was the one who had been circumcised. I knew, even beyond the books, what it would mean. I was a father. My decision about this would determine some part of his future forever. If it was true, as some books suggested, that sometimes the circumcised penis can grow insensitive to touch and sensation, making erections more difficult, then this decision could alter his sexual life forever. And yet there was the business of what to do with an uncircumcised penis – how to clean it, what to expect it to do or not to do. Here in this small matter, I was being thrust into fatherhood and it was not the most comfortable place in the world.

They placed Kekeli in a tray. I went closer to see him. I marvelled at the reptilian beauty of his face, his wetness and the purity of his skin. I was impressed by it all and grateful for his life. I could tell that it could have gone the other way when they pulled him out. When the doctor quickly reached for his neck, thrusting her fingers between the cord and his throat I could see that the umbilical cord was wound tightly around his frail neck. The nurses and assistants looked at me with a peculiar, serene quality of sympathy. I smiled back. Then they took him away, while drops were plopped into his eyes. I turned to Lorna, who was sleeping. The oxygen tape hung limply from her mouth. The doctor was chatting away to me as she sewed the incision, having drawn out and placed in a tray the cumbersome afterbirth. I tried to concentrate on what Dr. Anderson was saying, but in my head was only the loud declaration: "You have a son! You have a son!" It was not the noise of celebration, but a prophetic warning that threatened to overwhelm me.

They had feared that the sight of the Caesarean would make

me nauseous and faint and they warned me that once I was in the room, I could not leave. I was too worried about Lorna to really think about fainting, and Lorna, at that point, already groggy from the first anaesthetic injection, kept saying I should stay with her, stay with her. Throughout the operation, I was so fascinated by the process, by the light, the tinkling and glitter of the instruments, by the blood, and by that treacherous umbilical cord, that I had little time to feel faint or nervous. But now that the boy was born, now that Lorna was safe, now that my body was starting to calm, everything primordial – those chemicals raining in my blood – I began to feel a churning in my stomach, the seat of all my nervous tension. Dr. Anderson kept talking, the music of her Irishness sounding surreal in the now oppressive light. *You have a son!*

I moved like a zombie from the operating room to the nursery where Kekeli was being tagged, cleaned and given water. They let me touch him, hold him to me. I was not nervous here – Sena had been like this only a year before. He was light, delicate as a bird. He did all the appropriate things, clutching the finger, turning towards light, sniffing me. I put him down in the tray and left him there to do what babies do, live. Lorna would be out for several hours. Yes: circumcision – as soon as possible. Yes, breast feeding, so avoid any formula and the bottle for now, so that Lorna could feed him without any problems. His name. His names. Mawuena (I looked at a small notepad to confirm the spelling), Carlos Dawes.

I sat waiting for them to wheel Lorna into her room. It was still dark. Like Sena, Kekeli had come some time after midnight. Outside, Sumter was warm and thick with yellow pollen that clung to cars and clothes like the dustings of coloured powder at some Indian religious ceremony. My son was American. The completion of my move to this country had taken place, and in this moment I could not help but contemplate what it all meant. We had playfully considered the notion of leaving the

164

country for his birth – to Canada, England, Jamaica, anywhere. But we could never afford something like that, and we grudgingly acknowledged that perhaps this new citizenship for him would mean options, a certain freedom of movement, certain rights. This rationalization was coming from a part of me that had long been silenced. It was a pragmatism that came with fatherhood, a manner of projecting all decisions into the future – not my future, but the future of my children.

Sitting in that hospital room, waiting for Lorna, I really began to frighten myself with the implications of being father to an American boy. When they brought her in she was still completely under the anaesthetic. I wiped her forehead. I loved her so intensely at that moment, so powerfully that it confused me. I have no language for this cliché of emotion. Perhaps it was a fundamentally sexist instinct, a primordial, patriarchal instinct that makes a man feel intense love – pure, nonsexual love – for the woman who has given birth to his child. Whatever its roots, the sensation was hard to ignore. I touched her as the television sent bursts of colour through the darkened room. There was no volume, just the flickering light.

I went to get some water and ice for her to have when she woke up. On the way, it occurred to me to check on the baby. This time I watched him through the glass window, like they do on television. I stared at his tiny body, his sedate breathing. He was born, and a world of history would be carried in him, in that body, that tiny body. A son!

As I pictured the future I though of my relationship with my father, invariably complex and always marked by a sense of incompleteness. I was afraid of having a son because I was afraid of the inevitable battle between us that would come. All the ingredients were in place for this battle. I worried about him, about what he would make of me, of my image, how he would remember me when he was older and able to wonder about who I was, what I had done, what I had left for him. I had thought these things when Sena was born, yet I always felt that she would be forgiving, that she would cherish me without bitterness or resentment. The thought of a son gave me no such assurance. It is not that I was ever resentful of my father or more unforgiving about his failings than my sisters were. But I feared that I would not have the language or the capacity to win over my son: another male. He would see through every trick of mine, he would know my every weakness, know every trick I would play, know my failings, and tell me of them. I had always hoped that with a woman the business of telling me of my failings would be gentler. I knew these were all myths, these anxieties, these generalizations.

It didn't take long to realize that worrying about my legacy in that way was futile. At first we tend to assume that our children are small versions of us when they are so young. In time we come to realise that they are distinct, individual, and part of our life with them involves getting to know who they are. Kekeli, the infant, was a symbol for me of the upheaval of fatherhood, but Kekeli, the individual, would quickly become a fascinating new person in our lives. Still, the weight of his arrival, its significance, held me in thought as I made my way back to Lorna's room.

In the two hours that followed, while Lorna slept, I continued to think about the meaning of my fatherhood, to consider the fears I had. Recalling that time now, it is significant that I felt as if I was dragging out thoughts and fears that should be forgotten, quickly put away. I felt I should have left them in that hospital room, frightened away by the new sun of May 24, and by Lorna awakening, asking if it was a boy. I said yes. You have a son! I smiled wryly. Her eyes laughed at the recognition of my fear. She knew me.

CHAPTER 11

raising african american children

I have always felt that at the heart of the term, *African American*, there was both a lesson in resilience, defiance and affirmation, and a terrible tragedy that involved a capitulation that could at best be seen as an effort to minimise or compensate for the loss. The term has become solidly enshrined in American parlance over the past thirty years and appears to have become the preferred and official monicker for people of African descent in America. Well, not exactly. It depends on how far back the lineage of hyphenated descent goes.

America is full of hyphenated people. They can often trace their origins from their names, so that a surname can allow them to trace the family line to a small village in County Down or some hamlet in Germany, Switzerland or Italy. Typically, the European-American who does not know anything about his heritage outside America does not want to know.

In my classes, usually comprised of thirty to forty percent African Americans, I often ask the white students to talk about their origins. We go round the class and many of them will trace their families to Europe, to towns, and even villages, dating back centuries. They offer this matter-of-factly, not seeking to impress with their knowledge of this history and adamant that knowing that their ancestors were from Sicily has no impact on how they view themselves as entirely American today. Nonetheless, when I say the words, Italian-American, Greek-American, Irish-American, German-American or Polish-American, and ask them where people who refer to themselves as such are likely to have been born, they all agree that these are American-born individuals of some 'foreign' descent. But when I ask about Nigerian-Americans, Angolan-Americans or Ghanaian-Americans, they assume at once that these people were born in West Africa.

The significance of this difference does not become clear until I ask the African Americans in the class to trace back their origins to somewhere in Africa. They laugh, grow quiet and explain that they don't know. They only know *how* they came from Africa, know that this is where slaves came from and that people on that continent look like them. I ask them what the population of Nigeria is. They routinely underestimate by 80 - 100 million (It is 128 million). Africa is a small place in their minds. They begin to understand that even saying someone is a Nigerian-American is a massive generalisation. And none of them can even claim that.

Oprah Winfrey, until a DNA test told her otherwise, was long convinced by a myth she made up for herself that she was descended from the Zulu people of South Africa. It may have been her friendship with Nelson Mandela, or the new African American fascination with South Africa (a country that looks reassuringly modern and familiar) that birthed this myth, but it *was* a myth, an affirming myth of identity, but one that could only take root in the absence of genuine knowledge. It is a myth among many self-affirmative survival myths that have filled the space of the wilful and forced amnesia that was the experience of millions of descendants of enslaved people in the New World. Positively, the shift in naming signals that Africa is being embraced as a continent where once only a trait (the *Afro* as in Afro-American) was affirmed.

More and more people feel the need to return to the continent as a pilgrimage home. But these pilgrimages are often marked by sadness and disappointment. The "home" arrived at is uncertain. It is accepted as a matter of faith and a willed rejection of the systematic attempt to destroy any sense of history and dignity amongst black people.

This is why the name African American constitutes a symbol of defiance and an important shift in attitude towards Africa by many African Americans. But I know that I am not African American, not least because I am not quite American. I can certainly find a close affinity to that distinguished and complex presence, but at best I can only be grafted on to its legacy. My children, however, are closer to this line than I am. They are citizens. America, for the most part, is all they have known as home. They will have answers to their ancestry, at least on my Ghanaian side, but they must live in a culture that is shaped by the wrenching project of slavery. They, moreover, will have no claim to a home beyond America.

And my son is a black American, an African American. It does not take a journalist's inquisitive eye to know that being a black boy in America is a terribly complicated thing. Not long after I arrived in South Carolina, the statistics were all around me on television: black boys were at risk all over the country. Translation: black boys were more likely to be in jail or dead in much higher proportions, *much* higher, than any equivalent group. Even if the statistics were wrong, and even if the concentration of "at risk" blacks was geographically determined, what was most daunting to me was the national stereotype: young black males in their baggy trousers, with hip-hop pumping into their heads. These boys were walking problems: they were men before they could be boys, they were defined by an inner-city culture that was so pervasive and homogenising that it was pulling in rural youths, suburban youths, every kind of youth. It is easy to see how much we have all been sucked into the negative stereotype of the black boy. Just conjure up an image of him in your head. It is not, one can be sure, the image of a Tiger Woods.

Along with the image came the expectations and it was in these that I saw the greatest threat, the greatest danger for my son. It did not matter how well he behaved, or how well he did academically, the moment he acted in an angry manner or started to show any signs of that stereotype, he would quickly be slotted into the "hopeless" category and treated as such. I feared this fate because I had heard young black boys in Sumter complain again and again about such prejudiced attitudes. They would complain about not being understood because of their clothes or the way they talked. They talked about being suspended for reasons that seemed strange, because they were reasons that would lead only to a reprimand for a white boy. It was as if, they said, teachers were watching them closely, waiting for the fall to occur, for the bad side to kick in, as if this was a natural, albeit unfortunate, maturation process among black boys. At some point they, like fruit, would go bad. It was just a matter of time. This perception frightened me. What did such expectations do to the black boy growing up in America? Was it going to be possible to break such attitudes?

I began to think about what had given definition and meaning to my life while I was growing up, what had supplied me with a sense of control and self-assurance. In Jamaica I had lived in a country where there were still colonial remnants but whose leadership was ostensively pro-black and pro-African. I grew up at a time when Rastafarianism was on the rise and reggae was going international. Blackness, black identity was to be associated with intellect and imagination. I was among the majority and my sense of empowerment and self-esteem was tied up with this. Despite my strong claims to Ghana, I felt a sense of ownership in Jamaica. This was my space and I had the right to exist in it and inherit it fully.

I had not experienced, except through my imagination, the sense of disenfranchisement that came with being black in American society. For the black person in the USA to claim the society, claim the government, claim the landscape as belonging to him or her by right I saw as involving a leap of the imagination, an act of incredible nobility and bravery, but, nonetheless, fanciful. In a society whose commitment to the principles of majority power is so thorough, the minority person is constantly aware of his or her lack of power.

This became clear to me when I began to work at the Sumter campus of the University of South Carolina. During my second year there, three incidents made me feel a profound sense of helplessness and powerlessness as a black person. In each instance, I sought a way to kick back, but it was hard. I contemplated these things while I waited for Lorna to wake in the hospital. This was the world into which I was bringing this boy; I was going to father him in this society. I felt totally inadequate, totally.

That year, I had been asked to chair a committee established to plan an annual convocation for the beginning of the academic year. It was a good committee and I found the time planning the event quite rewarding. On the strength of some recommendations, the committee decided to ask a black poet, a South Carolinian living in Kentucky, to come and give the keynote speech. I did not know Nikky Finney at the time, but her credentials seemed solid enough and I liked the fact that she wore long, serious locks. I had no idea that her presence would cause problems.

She gave a powerful speech about "pluck", the capacity to speak up for what was right. It was intelligent, fiery, humorous, and sensitive. She was good. The students, I thought, had liked it very much; they had lined up to buy her book afterwards. But during the postmortem, it came out that many people had found her remarks too racial, too

171

much about being black. Some members of the committee reported that a number of students and faculty had complained about Finney's preoccupation with race. These were all white people who felt, somehow, left out, who felt that perhaps Finney had written a speech that was geared towards the minority – the blacks.

At first, I argued. I questioned the premise of these views; I sought to understand what specifically Finney had said that led to this conclusion. Nothing satisfactory was forthcoming – no details, no direct references to anything racial she may have said. I became quite annoyed at the weight given by the committee to these few dissenting views. I felt frustrated, tempted to give up and say that they were right, that this was a white world and a black woman speaking at their convocation was probably a mistake. I felt this to be my only recourse. I had tried reason, tried arguing that had the speaker been a white talking about hunting fox in the coastal area of the state, no one would have called the speech racially limiting. But my efforts were futile. There was no sense of irony, no humour – it was all quite disturbing. I began to want to take refuge in my alien status. It was a simple equation: "You blacks and whites in America have a serious challenge before you and that is integration. You want racial tolerance and a society marked by peaceful racial cohabitation. But you are fighting over the full recognition of Martin Luther King Jr. as a symbol of the country's racial aspirations. You are bickering about whether to recognize the King holiday for all Americans or just African Americans. You ask me to come and chair a committee that seeks to explore the interracial dynamics in the community. You want me to explore the reason why so many of your colleagues are fighting this holiday observance so vehemently." I had been tossed into the fray and asked to speak as if I was a representative African American and to offer them guidance. It was becoming my battle, this absurd debate about Martin Luther King Jr. Day. I did not want this to be my war and I felt free to assume a self-righteous distance, declaring this an American problem, an American race problem that, ultimately, had nothing to do with me.

But I was deceiving myself. It had everything to do with me and I had made sure of this from the moment I started to live in America. I wanted to find myself, to locate my sense of connection, to find a niche that made sense. I could see the slot I was being pushed into. When complicated racial conflicts, emerged, I was consulted. When committees were being drawn up to consider the holding of a Martin Luther King celebration, I was selected. When people wanted to know how to add more African-Americans to their course syllabi, I was asked. When it was important to show campus guests that there were blacks on the faculty, I was somehow co-opted into certain gatherings. This was benign tokenism but it was quite odd to me because I was expected to be black and American without any questions asked.

Indeed, one of the first times I was moved close to violence, actual violence, as a result of racial attitudes, involved not a white racist, but a black man. He was something of an eccentric who fancied himself a writer and was in the habit of latching onto writers to explore the possibilities of his own writing career. But he was also a mentally unstable man who complicated his notoriety in Sumter by being a flamboyant and public cross-dresser. I knew none of this when I first met him in my new office at the university. A colleague had sent him to me. Apparently, he had been pestering her for years and she felt unable to communicate with him. She assumed it was a racial problem. Despite the fact that I was completely new to America, the assumption was made that I was an expert on black American life. I was expected, then, to know how to handle maverick African-American, cross-dressing, aspiring writers.

We were immediately in conflict. His aim was to educate

me because he was American and I, an African, would be ignorant about most things. I was patient until he began to offer America as the epitome of all that is good, and Africa of all that is bad.

"So why can't those people in Africa be like us? Why can't they learn to build and farm and be great? They just killing each other, those Africans." He spoke as if he was reprimanding me for Africa's woes.

"When you say 'us', who do you mean?" I asked, trying to temper my growing impatience.

"Americans. We are the greatest country in the world. We get along, people of all races. We have found peace."

"You live in the South and you say this?" I asked.

"Africans, I have seen them. They have no confidence. You could learn from us." He was preaching again.

"What Africans do you know?" I asked.

"They are killing each other on TV everyday. That never happens here. Never happens."

"So Blacks are quite fine in America, always have been?" I knew that sarcasm would be quite futile, but I offered it as a stopgap to my agitation.

"You were fortunate. You see how educated you are? You got in and got an education and look at you now. America..."

"I was not educated in America..." I said slowly. "You ever thought that maybe your Sumter education is part of why you are still struggling to get anything in life? You ever think maybe things would be easier for you without..." But he was not listening. He was actually feeling sorry for me.

"Africans should look at us..."

I lost it then. I told him to look at his America, to see what part he had in it, what it had done to his people and determine whether it was all good. I told him he was ignorant and needed to leave my office before I became violent. I was angry and I sensed that my anger was exacerbated by the fact that he was black. There was no affinity between us. I was a foreigner. I may have looked like him, but it stopped at that.

But I had at first walked into the slot as if it was the most natural space for me. I was connected to America, to black America; I had been for most of my life. I remember understanding the completely American character of Muhammed Ali, whom I had supported with total loyalty and awe. It was as simple as that; the enemies of his people were my enemies as well.

Angela Davis was another hero. Her picture, with that explosive Afro, was part of me, integral to my image of black assertion, of fierce womanhood, and mythic struggle against bigotry. Angela Davis was, in my imagination, part of the America I was somehow connected to.

And there were Martin Luther King Jr., Malcolm X and Sidney Poitier. There were Harry Belafonte, Cecily Tyson and, later, Alex Haley. These people with their narratives were part of my imagination along with the images of the Civil Rights Movement laid out before me in *Life* photospreads. I knew whose side I was on. The dogs were leaping at the ones who looked like me. The world of Black America, the music, the television shows – these were the points at which America made sense to many of us in Jamaica. There was no way for me to see *Roots* and not find a strong emotional affinity to the black American experience.

When *Roots* was aired in Jamaica in the mid seventies, it rhymed well with the songs of Burning Spear, The Mighty Diamonds, Culture, Dennis Brown and Bob Marley, songs I knew by heart, songs that filled me with a palpable sense of history. I saw the tale of Kunta Kinte as my own story. Nation did not matter. Quincy Jones' elegant soundtrack was used as the setting for the National Dance Theatre Company's beautifully complex 'The Crossing', a dance drama that bridged any divide there might have been between African American and African

Caribbean experience. *Roots* was the visualization of what we were learning in West Indian history at school. Slavery was not distant history for me. We had visited the Rose Hall Plantation in St. Ann, Maroon Town in the Cockpit Country and the Institute of Jamaica museum in Kingston where shackles and other instruments of torture from slavery days were on display.

Since *Roots* I had seen more and more films about African American life that entrenched my sense of affinity to that culture's history. I was twenty-four when I saw the film made of Alice Walker's *The Color Purple*; I sat in the lofty balcony of an empty theatre watching the film. Outside, Kingston was being its mad self. In the huge theatre, alone, in the middle of the day, I wept through a drama that I felt was wholly connected to me. I was drawn by the narrative, the Hollywood hooks, the clichés and, above all, by the poetry of the telling. It made me weep over the language of the art that took pain and created beauty. I would later come to see this as a Blues paradigm, but at the time it just made sense to me. In America, I would be black first.

But in this country, you have to uncover something deeper than the myths of film and television. The people are real, present, and suddenly the written history seems trite – the history you know does not gel with what you sense in the coded language between the races. Or perhaps, down in Sumter, it was a mistrust of the assumption that things had changed; my feeling that despite the absence of signs reading "Whites Only" or "No Coloreds", two hundred years of sophisticated social engineering could not simply vanish in twenty years. I kept looking into the faces of the older whites to see traces of that past. Someone must have picketed the desegregating schools; someone must have donned the pointed hat and sheet of the Klan; someone must have fired workers for marching to Selma or Washington; someone must have seethed at the unearthing of Civil War memories – that spitting on the graves of the old Confederate soldiers; someone must have argued vehemently for the white flight from the public schools after blacks began to darken the classrooms of their children; someone must have gathered to watch the beaten body of a black man dangle in the russet sunrise of the swamp; someone must have smiled ruefully when the photographs of Andrew Young and Jesse Jackson, pointing to some ghost in the dark, appeared in the newspaper; someone walking on these roads, someone in this town, someone. I was obsessed with the question of how, or even whether, time could change the person who was brought up to accept the rituals and advantages of racism.

It was inevitable, even in the absence of any clear evidence, that powerful images of Southern racism were part of my consciousness during my first days in this world. I was wary and worried about it, I must have been. On my first day at the university in Sumter, I decided to walk home, walk to our apartment on Alice Drive. We had no car and, besides, I could not drive. I was lost immediately, and I panicked. It was late in the afternoon and gloomy. I found myself walking beside a thick forest of impenetrable vegetation on Alice Drive. Traffic moved in sputters, each car light filling me with relief and uncertainty. I was afraid. It is amusing to consider this now, for I now know Alice Drive and I know Sumter and I know that racial violence does not randomly leap at you in broad daylight. But as I walked that evening, my armpits prickled with anxiety. I imagined being jumped upon, beaten, dragged into the bushes, and left for dead. I did. And in the midst of that, a loud explosion behind me filled my whole body with terror. I was almost in the bushes in my shock, convinced I had been shot at, convinced that one of the millions of guns on the streets of America had exploded behind me and wanted to take my life. Then I heard the laughter and saw an open-bodied Jeep full of teenage boys hurtling past; they were looking back at me and laughing. I started. They laughed some more and I felt completely helpless, a useless network of tattered nerves. I was afraid. I arrived home uncertain of what to say, what to do. Nothing had happened and yet something had happened in me. I needed to know.

I needed to know what living as a black in the South meant. I knew that it meant living with a history. I also knew that the very negative images of whiteness that had suggested themselves to me from my reading and viewing had to be scrutinized with suspicion. It had to be far more complicated than this Manichean arrangement of monsters and victims that was in my head. It is not that the history of race, of slavery, of segregation had not interested me in Jamaica; it had. But race in Jamaica was different, was made strangely complicated by the interracial mix, by the fact that it was hard to find any "pure" white in Jamaica, any white person who did not show some evidence that a compromise of sorts had taken place along racial lines. Resentment over lightness of skin is, in Jamaica, predominantly an issue of class. Tracing a light-skinned Jamaican's history to some plantation owner who owned slaves was also about tracing that history to the slaves themselves – the blood of both ran in the veins and this did not make anger or resentment towards those who were lighter skinned easy or satisfying. The anger I felt as a thirteen year old when I learned about slavery was only briefly directed at the light-skinned boys in my class.

There were, indeed, dramatic epiphanies in our study of West Indian history, and a fantastic awakening of consciousness when we studied slavery, emancipation, and rebellion in class. There was the tense silence of anger and deep resentment felt by many black boys after learning about the amputation of the feet of slaves when they tried to escape. I still remember the discomfort of the fair-skinned boys. I recall the accusatory stares, the growing unease, and a peculiar realization that vengeance was sweet and compelling and that it cut across the generations.

Our history teacher showed us pictures of the skeletons of

blacks found on old plantations, feet chopped at the ankle, hands chopped off at the wrists, the missing members lost forever, tossed to some stray mongrel who had gnawed the soft bone into manure; this in a classroom of boys of many hues. There were in the room two very white boys. They sat listening. Maybe they felt the same sense of outrage that we did, but I recall the way in which many of the black boys began to look at these two white friends, boys we had played cricket with and lied with about our sexual exploits, and now, suddenly, they were transformed into the enemy. We wanted to take revenge. We wanted to finish the fight that Juan de Bolas had lost, that Cudjoe had lost, that Tacky had lost. Someone shouted out: "It's all you people" pointing to the white boys, and no one laughed. The teacher tried to continue. We were not listening. Maybe two minutes passed in silence. We were all waiting. The white boys wanted to go – we sensed that – but they did not know where to go. Then someone laughed. "Jesus, Macky, you look frighten nuh hell!" And somehow we could all laugh at that. And we laughed and laughed and laughed until the class ended and we went outside and played scrimmage all together as if nothing had happened. But somewhere deep inside we knew that something painful had happened. We had encountered history and found we could not change it. We had met the past and discovered that the present had made the easy moral demarcation far more complex. Yet we could not simply accept the history as something to get over. This history meant something about the way we lived now. From then on we all said together that we would watch and pray that nobody did the same evil that was done to us again...

It was clear enough to me, though, that the white boys could also claim the same anger, the same resentment for that system. They too had ancestors who would have been slaves and, even more, they represented the truth about miscegenation and rape that occurred in slave society. Their mixed race position implied

179

violence. And were I to be honest about the evidence of my racial inheritance, I would have to admit that a few generations into my father's lineage there were 'thoroughbred' whites. My grandmother was very light-skinned, and her parents – one of them, I am sure, was a white person, or at least close to it. I too had the trace of complicity in my veins. I claimed my blackness, yes, but I could not be angry without denying the complication of my blood.

None of this should be taken to imply that Jamaican blacks are more "mixed" than African Americans. They are not. But where the "single drop" theory of white supremacy dominated American race relationships, it only held sway in Jamaica during its earlier history. But even given my own racial mix, I have to say that I do not feel any especial affinity to my white ancestry, nor does knowing it exists in any way undermine my self-identification with being black and African. Indeed, growing up in Jamaica in the 1970s played a major role in shaping my sense of blackness, even if the objects of anger were not as easily available or as "pure" as they would have been in the US.

America presented another pattern, one in which the pretence of "purity" was basic to the way people lived. Whites were white. Blacks, even those who showed the smallest sign of being of mixed race, were black. The implication was simple: whites descended from the planter, the privileged class (or at least those who had not been slaves) and blacks descended from slaves. If whites were indeed "passing" it was clearly not to be announced. The implication was full of problems; not all whites had owned slaves, for instance. Yet whites and blacks live in a very clearly defined hierarchy of value, which was predicated on the simple equation that whites, as a class, had once been owners of blacks. Racial demarcations, then, were real in this world I had entered. When I saw a white whose family had lived in the South for generations, I saw a lineage that lead directly to the business of slavery. I wanted to understand how that fact affected the present. I was not sure what it all meant. I knew, though, that I was sceptical about the suggestion that all had changed in twenty years.

So I started some informal research. I pulled out historical texts on the South, the Civil War, slavery, and social organizations that dealt directly with Sumter. I went even farther back to the Revolutionary War, trying to trace the name Sumter. I found General Sumter, a maverick Revolutionary War soldier, the man whose name the town bears. It was all swashbuckling and bloody, but it barely began to help me grasp the world I was living in. Yes, there was slavery; yes, segregation was quite strong in this society; yes, the Klan did its nasty work here too; yes, there were Jim Crow laws; yes, South Carolina was a bastion of the Confederate cause and for upholding the old tradition of racial superiority. There were no surprises and I became more obsessed with the family names of whites that littered the pages. I imagined lineage. I even asked a few students about their family histories. I found this manner of linking the past and the present to be satisfying, yet I realized that I was still trying to answer a question that these books could not answer. What was going on in the minds of African Americans in light of this history? I was supposed to be black, yet I did not really know it, not like they did. I had read, yes, but I did not know it in the people I lived among.

In less than two years we would have another American child. Now whatever my relationship to America may have been, it was now complicated by two crucial transforming facts: 1) I had now lived in America long enough to see it as home and 2) I now had American children who were working out the meaning of that fact and the fact of their parents' origin for themselves.

So the next ten years would be spent carrying out the rituals of making South Carolina our home. The need for stability for the children's education made this a necessity. So we would buy a house, then move to another, enact the business of decorating it, working on the yard, planning for the years when the children would leave home for university, finding a church where we could transform ourselves from visitors to members, active and rooted.

CHAPTER 12

going to church

Choosing a church for ourselves was a serious priority when we arrived in South Carolina, but we were determined to resist the patterns of racial segregation in the churches. This would prove complicated, an almost impossible task given the social importance of the church in the South. Churches are, quite simply, the last hold-out of the segregated South and there is a fascinating complicity between blacks and whites in sustaining this divide. Their reasons are quite clearly different, but the rationales offered, embraced as a given by many church leaders and organisations in the South, point to the same issue. The churches are segregated because blacks and whites are so culturally different that they can't worship comfortably together. Whites and blacks engage in only slightly euphemistic stereotypes (which would normally offend) when they talk about it. Blacks are more passionate, full of rhythm and like to make a joyful noise and express themselves. Translation: noisy, uncontrolled, flamboyant, and crude. On the other hand, whites are reflective, quiet, organized, and regimented in their worship. Translation: dead, dull, lacking in emotional commitment. These are the cultural "differences" offered. So blacks won't go to white churches because they are not lively enough for them and whites won't go to black churches because they are too lively for their tastes. I am constantly amazed at how openly these stereotypes are uttered by people who feel they are being generous and completely sincere in what they are saying.

Such assertions cover up a multitude of sins and we began to see the sins as we struggled with the question of where to establish our fellowship. At first we searched through the Yellow Pages to find churches that did not appear to be heavily traditional or strictly denominational. The phrase 'nondenominational' is often a code word for several things, some positive and some not. On the one hand, it suggests a church that is in some way connected to the Charismatic movement; a movement that spawned the church we attended in Jamaica. Sometimes, it also connotes a church willing to break the practices of racial segregation. However, some such churches are often small, single-pastored units, sometimes holding rather strange and questionable doctrines conjured up by the imagination of that single pastor. Such churches also tend to have to find ways to justify their existence. The options are limited. A man (or woman) decides that he or she has received some new and unique revelation from God. He or she concludes that he or she needs to establish a church in which to pass on this great news. These are the signs of potential demagoguery, or egomania in the desire to plant a church and to start a movement – this in a State that is cluttered with churches of every conceivable ilk. Sometimes, these churches are established for largely commercial reasons, a sad truth about the growth of small (and large) independent churches around America. The economics are sometimes so inextricably linked to the notions of mission, calling, and spiritual mandate that even the best intentioned pastors can trick themselves into believing that they must have their own fellowship to lead and guide in God's will. But they are often simply small business entrepreneurs trying to hustle a living.

We saw many such churches as we began to move around each Sunday, searching for a fellowship. We entered small storefront churches, with metal chairs and pulpits of deeply secular mundaneness, the windows covered with thin, bright curtains. There was always a tiny organ – a Yamaha or a Casio with that thin, mechanical sound. These churches held no appeal to us because of the youth of their leaders and the youth of their experience as churches. They were often mixed-race fellowships, but they were often so proud of the fact, so excessively self-congratulatory about their uniqueness, that it aroused one's suspicions.

Many of the black churches were thoroughly black: lively places with dynamic leaders and loud if not gifted choirs. It did not take us long to sniff out the self-involved nature of some of these leaders. We avoided these churches because we feared that we would spend so much energy finding fault, second-guessing unwise statements and acts, that we would become quite hopeless members. So we decided to try the white churches. The completeness of the whiteness amazed us. These were old churches dating back generations. Pews were almost owned in the nineteenth century sense and it did not take us long to realize that we would be a challenge to that kind of church; a challenge that would make us feel uncomfortably self-conscious of our difference.

But why would we choose to attend a white church? To usher in a new era of desegregation? To act as leaders, to integrate all the white churches in the city? We felt no such calling and could not pretend that this would be our quixotic motive. For us, as for the rest of the black community (an actual entity when you live in a southern town), our decision would be about pulling away from blackness and towards whiteness – an act of racial self-denial. Many expected this of me. I was a professor in a university that was not known for its interest in hiring African Americans as faculty – a white school despite the number of black students who attended. For me to be there suggested that the whites who hired me saw me as less black than most blacks; saw me as easily managed. It would stand to reason, then, that I would be the kind of person who would be most comfortable in the world of black denial of the white church. By going to a white church, I would alienate myself from the black community, and I had no intention of doing anything of that kind.

Needless to say, both whites and blacks expected that we would attend a black church. And while our concern about segregation was equally applicable to the all-black fellowships, it was, somehow, less disruptive for us to slide past *those* racial demarcations and find our way in *that* world. Either route was uncomfortable to someone who was not convinced of the validity of segregated worship.

I wondered what this pattern of segregation would do for our children's sense of themselves and their understanding of race in their lives. Segregation is strangely seductive; in the South, it is often the easiest path. It is no longer entirely a matter of whites denying blacks access, but is, in many instances, a mutual agreement, a pact of sorts that says, "We will do our thing and you will do yours." I realized, after talking to a number of blacks and whites, that the reasons for wanting to continue with this segregation differed along racial lines. There are points at which they overlap, particularly in the area that is euphemistically referred to as "cultural differences", but for the most part, the segregation and the reasons for it are disturbing indications of how race still functions in the South.

Whites regard the church they have attended all their lives as family. This is no small thing. These people have grown up together, their parents and grandparents have all grown up in these churches. They have married in these churches, been baptized there, blessed there, and buried there. They have left to live in sin and returned to live in repentance and die in grace. They

186

have paid dearly for the building, invested in its beauty and protected its reputation. Where these churches have church schools, they have sent their children there and have invested in the schools financially and with time. The phrase "my church" is not a small claim; it is a claim of ownership, of family ownership. Race is clearly implied in that context: Blacks are not family. Blacks would not be turned away from these churches, but blacks would know quickly that they are not part of the tradition, part of the family memory. The truth is that many of the older whites in these churches were determined racists who fought to maintain white ascendancy in the South. Many may regret their actions, but not enough to see the need to change the constitution of their fellowship. The fact that the church was the one place for which racial integration could not be legislated meant that, for many whites, protecting the purity of the church was the last bastion against the push towards integration.

No one has forgotten the white churches' collusion with the segregated past. Any move towards integration would mean a confrontation with that past. It would involve the kind of self-exposure that no one feels comfortable doing. It would challenge the very right to make decisions about whom to relate to, whom to associate with in life. Christian doctrine has little to do with it. It is entirely social and political. It has to do with the same spirit that makes many whites determined to keep the confederate flag flying over the State House in the capital. In their eyes it is not a matter of race, but a question of tradition, a cry to remember those who died defending that flag. To remove the flag would be to suggest that those who fought to defend it, to defend a way of life not loved by the hypocritical North, were somehow morally bereft. It is a twisted piece of logic but it remains as irrational and emotionally charged a feeling as the desire to maintain a segregated church.

In the mid-nineties, a few black and white church leaders in Sumter were, in one denomination, offered the chance to pro-actively integrate their churches. This denomination proposed a system whereby the pastor of a black church would spend six months to a year serving as pastor for a white church. A white pastor would serve in a black church for the same period. I learned of this project from a white pastor: an older, thin and seemingly world-weary man, who was a student on a religious studies course. I was asked to give a lecture to this class. I spoke about African religions, but the discussion shifted to the church in the South. He spoke slowly, in an un-pastor-like way, but with the strange assurance of deeply Southern whites, who speak with an authority that can sometimes be intimidating. He was of the ilk, too, that take a special pride in trying to make a black man, any black man, understand that they had no right to feel privileged or superior to whites. I had met several such whites as a professor and as a consultant with the local government. These men always felt the need to let me know that they were not impressed with my education and big-talking ways. They always made it clear that I would have to know the blacks in the South, *their* blacks, before I could speak with any sense about race. They spoke to me with an air of condescension and with the suggestion that they felt I could not know very much about anything.

In this lecture, I must have made some strong statement about the tragedy of segregation in the church and the racism in the white church. I wondered why the churches could not be integrated. This is when he spoke up or, rather, shouted: "Now let me tell you something, young fella..." He told of the project that was put to him. He smiled and explained that he had told the person proposing this idea that he would never let a black man take his pulpit. He stopped, as if it were enough that he had said this. I asked him why he wouldn't. He thought for a second or two and then said, "'Cause Ah wouldn't have me a congregation, then. Not after that." But he was not pushing the blame on the church as a way to extricate himself from the position. He was clear that he would agree with the members. They would leave, he said. All leave. They would never allow themselves to be pastored by a black man, even temporarily.

I wanted to ask him if it might not be appropriate to God's cause if the disgruntled members did leave. But I didn't, because I knew the answer. Churches, regardless of their noble purpose, depend, in this country, on money, on the gifts of members. It has always been that way, I suppose, but in Paul's day, things were still so loose that Paul could conceive of himself as someone willing not to take money from a church for his upkeep. Not today. This man knew that the oldest families would leave and they would be the wealthiest families. If they left, there would be no money, no salary for the leader, no mortgage payment on the building, no money for utilities – nothing. It would be disastrous, the demise of a church. And for what? Was it worth it? Was it worth it for me to face all the headaches of attending a white church just to make a point that would be consumed by the clutter of my life? For this pastor it was a "no-brainer". Integration was a bad idea. He ended by saying that, "Anyway, our cultures are different." I asked him to explain and he dismissed the question as absurd.

A black pastor in that class also spoke. He, too, would resist integration, but for far different reasons, even if they *were* related to the same issue of money. To what end, he wondered, was this move for pastoral exchanges? If the ultimate aim was the full integration of the churches by amalgamation, he would object. Integration, he feared, would put him out of work. If the church was integrated, who would get the pastoral jobs? And here is where money came in. Since, as the white pastor said, the whites would all flee at the prospect of a black pastor, and since blacks would have no problem with a white pastor, as they were long used to white leadership in most other aspects of their lives, the black pastor would be both a financial liability and financially vulnerable. To maintain its funding, the church would wisely turn to a white pastor, regardless of his abilities. Black pastors, he said, knew this. They knew that the economics of race made integration deadly for their career advancement and security.

It is not cynical to suggest that these financial issues have played a part in shaping the racial dynamics in the church. It is one part of the dilemma. The other is simple racism – the desire to stay separate, on both sides. Too much water under the bridge, both sides say. I wonder how I will explain this state of affairs to my children. I know I will have to show them the reality of a segregated world, show them that the rituals of race have become tied to the rituals of absolute truth and absolute morality. Without that honesty, the world would be a far too complicated and cynical a place. But I have worried about this, worried about the ineffectuality of the segregated churches, worried about the safe world of the familiar that it would all point to.

Of course, the race dilemma in the church is not just a matter for the white churches. In the same way that they are family shelters, the same is true of many black churches. Indeed, because these churches emerged in a hostile environment, a world in which the very humanity of blacks was challenged on a biblical basis, the tradition of the black church is one of survival and sublime triumph against the greatest odds. These churches helped to sustain the family, the community, the civility and the culture of African Americans in the South. Their songs are not just different in sound and rhythm, but are rooted in a history that evokes emotional and psychic connections that are profoundly spiritual, even as they are rooted in the pragmatics of life.

In the black church, the black man and woman, the black gardener, the black sharecropper, the black maid, the black chauffeur, had position, dignity and respect; was more than a 'boy', was more than a nanny, an 'auntie' or 'uncle'. In the church he or she was a person who did things that gained respect and appreciation. The church was a shelter, a place of rest in which the psychological battlefield of a Jim Crow existence (and all its less overt descendants) was removed, at least for a little while. To suggest that such a church is in any sense 'wrong' in protecting itself as a black institution is a deeply troubling idea, and one that I think emerges from a failure to understand the nature of its history.

This is something that many of us, blacks who have recently come to America, have tended to do. I, certainly, did not properly understand the role of the black church. After all, the bible offers clear evidence that the gospel came to expunge enmity between people, to do away with segregation by race and culture, to propose instead a new world of brotherhood that annihilates such divisions. So, I was uncomfortable about attending an all-black church because I felt that this simply fed into the sin of segregation.

In Sumter we attended a black episcopal church led by a Jamaican priest who became a close friend. It was a small church and largely middle-class in its congregation. We felt comfortable forgoing our our evangelical faith largely because of the Jamaican priest and his family and other friends we found in the church.

However, we continued to search. Eventually, we found a mixed-race fellowship. But even here, we were constantly aware that the church was wrestling with its own racial ambivalences. It was not hard to see it, at core, as a white church that was open to blacks. We began to understand better the heavy price that had to be paid to forge a multiracial environment in a community that had not been accustomed to such a culture in its past. But at least it was a church that was trying to do something. I was grateful for what that meant for my children. At least for one day they saw people of all different races doing something intimate together. That was important. And yet I knew that many whites in this church worried that this spiritual integration would lead to the ultimate act of integration: marriage between the races. People still married within the church but would white members be comfortable with their children dating interracially? I know that the dynamics of race in the South will make such an eventuality deeply troubling and dangerous for my own children. But I could not, simply on the basis of race, resist such a thing, not in good conscience. And yet, I wonder whether it is possible, in such a racially charged world, for love to be devoid of strange, self-deprecating assessments of one's own race and colour, or of the power-politics of race – white superior to black, etc.; I do wonder.

At church, we were struck by the way race affects the relationships in the fellowship, the manner in which intimacies are established or not established. We were struck by stories of long-standing "friendships" between blacks and whites which are still carefully mitigated by the rituals of racial distance, where "friends" live very separate private lives and conversations about racial matters are never broached. A white acquaintance confessed to us that she would not deal openly with any issue concerning race with her black friend: it was just not part of their friendship to resolve racial differences. But they are committed to their friendship in a strange act of faith – blind faith. It is almost as if in the church a peculiar contract has been drawn up which suggests that, if ignored, racial problems will go away. Many whites seem fatigued by the burden of race and the feeling that they have been asked to carry the responsibility for racism for far too long. They feel that they have done enough, said enough "I'm sorrys" and are now trying to avoid the matter altogether.

In the church, though, there is an added dimension. Much of charismatic teaching about faith is founded on the notion of "claiming" what is true in the "spirit world", even if the temporal world denies that "truth". The principle is that "faith is the substance of things hoped for", but more crucially, the writer of the book of Hebrews' additional construction ("The evidence of things not seen") speaks to the idea of looking not at the symptoms, but at the articulation of truth in the spiritual realm. Thus, if, in faith, one has accepted that racism is defeated and does not have any place in the church, then it is incumbent on the faith-filled believer to reject the possibility that symptoms of racism may exist in the church. To acknowledge these symptoms would be tantamount to denying the capacity of God to heal this problem. The dynamic can grow more complicated, because this whole approach leads to the denial, as an almost pathological fixation, of any counter-evidence for what is believed as a matter of faith, and Christian faith in such a charismatic context can be so emotionally defining, so ingrained in the meaning of self and the meaning of one's salvation, that denial of the existence of failure, sin or the absence of healing becomes glorified as a sign of faithfulness.

It is a false but handy assurance because when the symptoms *can* be ignored, when they do not debilitate in obvious ways (like being wheelchair-ridden or ravaged by cancer) it is easy, and sometimes quite desirable, to ignore them. At best, this manner of regarding racial problems in the church is an act of wishful thinking, a self-delusion. At worst, it is a cynical way of perpetuating the old racist order of things.

We sat in church and watched people avoid race like battle-weary combatants, too shell-shocked to want to say anything about it, too uncertain of themselves and the potential consequences of venturing out with a challenge or a question. The fear was that broaching the topic was not worth the suffering that could come as a consequence. But with such classic denial there was no change of behaviour. Race still defined behaviour in the church. In that mixed race church we attended in Columbia for seven years, whiteness remained the cultural norm and black culture was an aberration.

Our pastor was a committed older man who had come a long way in his own dealings with race. He was proud of the bi-racial or multiracial nature of the church. But he came from an entirely white evangelical background and held to the dubious view that when he saw people he did not see their race, he just saw people. This is "faith" talking. It is a good faithful articulation. In truth, what he may have been saying is that when he saw black people he did not see black people but saw versions of white people. The danger in this construction is that blacks functioned in the church fully aware of the expectation that they would adopt a more Southern white culture and suppress their own Southern black culture in the process. This was the way to bring peace and harmony. An act of total self-denial and sacrifice.

One afternoon, we had over some friends from the church. They were leaders in the church. Our talk turned to race issues and one of our friends, one of the few black leaders in the church, was waxing eloquent about a newly appointed youth pastor, who was white, who had replaced a black youth pastor who had departed under rather tense circumstances. Our black friend declared with passion about the new leader, "He has not an ounce of prejudice in his blood!" It was hard to even start to accept this notion from our friend who had, earlier that afternoon, suggested that the pastor who had left may have had a tendency to be *too* black. It was an oblique reference to his view of how black people can do well in the church. He said that those who came in without carrying with them all this "blackness stuff" got along with everybody and were good people for the church. I understood his assertion as expressing his own struggle to gain a foothold in the church. He'd had to compromise. He'd had to discard much of the "blackness stuff" which alienated and intimidated whites, and assume a manner that was more comfortable for them. This was the price he'd had to pay to be where he was in the church. This saddened me, even more so because he saw this as an appropriate way of dealing with the wider dynamics of race. Was this what Paul, the apostle, meant by "being all things to all men" so that he might win them to the Lord? Surely, it would be hard not to see one's "blackness" as a negative thing in such a situation.

Would saying anything about it amount to carrying around all this "black stuff"? Does acceptance in the church mean suppressing any overt show of blackness – American blackness, that is? And what would be these signs of blackness? A desire to hear more black music in the services? A passionate exuberance in worship? An articulated desire to see more blacks in leadership? An assertion that even in the church racial discrimination and prejudice exist and thrive? We did not ask what this "black stuff" was, what he meant by it, but we worried that we were somewhere on the right track.

In the church, albeit an integrated church, whiteness is the norm and white long-standing members panic when blackness becomes more visible. Here blackness is largely American blackness because my brand of blackness is exotic and can easily be put in its rightful place. American blackness, on the other hand, is so completely inscribed in the imagination of white society that whereas reggae would be an acceptable musical form to play around with in this integrated church, rap music would be a huge problem – too black. The truth is that most of the members of the church would not attend a church that was culturally black. They would say, as the pastor had said, that this was outside their culture, their sense of who they were. On the other hand, blacks are somehow able to sit in churches where white culture dominates, even when they are not entirely inscribed in white culture and its practices. Thus, in our church, I witnessed the basic pattern of integration in the South.

Three years ago, we decided to move to another church, a black Baptist church. The pastor is from Tanzania, and the multi-national nature of the church, along with the promise of activities for the children, prompted our move. But at the heart of our decision to leave our former, largely white church was our embroilment in its race dynamics. It was a painful move, marked by a growing sense that race can be a more insurmountable barrier to Christian fellowship than one could have imagined. We left somewhat defeated because we, too, had succumbed to the pressure of segregation. In this instance, it was clear that being black in a predominantly white Southern church was often a pained place to be, a place in which misunderstandings can occur, in which the legacies of slavery and race still find a way to colour and complicate the interactions between people; a place where fresh wounds can be made and old wounds re-opened. We chose a more pragmatic path – a conventional one. In an African-American church we found ourselves breathing easier – not so much because of how things were done, but because we did not have to negotiate race in everything we did. We are still foreigners in America, but being among blacks can be a refuge, a safe place after spending most of one's week working through the minefields of race. I understand now why the South can make segregation so comfortable, so normal, so reasonable. It is a false security, and it is also a tragic truth that the status-quo is only effectively challenged through the sometimes unreasonable practices of idealism and principle.

To have stayed in the former church might have been a principled act, a gesture of idealism, and one that would have cost dearly in emotional pain, spiritual trauma and, arguably, greater racial disquiet and tension. Yet moving, too, was principled: an acceptance of defeat and a sincere feeling that the core values of our faith were being overrun by the pressures of a racial legacy that could not be ignored.

The longer I live in this country, the more I start to be seduced by the ease of compromise and compliance. Faith in this context becomes a prompting to constant reassessments. I still don't know how we can be so segregated and worship the same God. I still don't know why it is not seen as a terrible sin. But I do know that I, too, have become part of a culture that allows this to be the norm. It is how one becomes American.

CHAPTER 13

the 'talk'

Now that we are in its trenches, it is clear that parenting in America will bring some challenges. We are parenting American children, but were not brought up as Americans and are not yet American citizens. There is much about America that we admire, but also a great deal that we do not like.

Our biggest challenge in parenting as immigrants is the absence of a community with which we can share the burden. There is no Jamaican or even a significant Caribbean community here in Columbia that could, as happens in many other larger cities, reinforce the cultural expectations we place on our children. We have few family and friends from Jamaica who can identify with our cultural expectations and hang-ups. There are few people to whom we can complain about those strange Americanisms that bother us. Functioning in isolation, we sometimes feel beleaguered. The isolation brings problems which often have less to do with race than culture. Sometimes we find more immediate affinity with non-black, non-Americans than with black Americans. This is a problem because we are black in America and our children are African Americans. Right at the heart of our family life and the developing identities of our children, we have to deal with the relationship between America and the rest of the world.

Every parent has to look to their childhood experience for models of parenting to be embraced or rejected. In America, without the reinforcement of a community that shares our values, this task of evaluation becomes particularly acute. As parents, we are constantly having to balance between an inclination to draw from our Jamaican/British/Ghanaian pasts, and the pressure to change these ideas to fit our lives in America. It is already apparent that some things that were not important in our childhoods will need more care and attention here in the USA. The range of such things is quite extensive and we are still not sure whether we know how we will deal with them. I am still learning how to give the series of "talks" we must have with our children at some point in their lives. We recognise that the "talk" is the quintessential American mode of parenting: The Sex Talk, The Drugs Talk, The God Talk, The Race Talk and so on. We are still discovering what should be on our list because we did not have "talks" while growing up. Could we get away without them in America?

There is something about America that forces you to contend with your own prejudices and biases, things that remain theoretical when you live in places where race is more subtly enacted. As children in Jamaica, like most people living in a world permeated by American television, American pop culture and American fantasy, I and my siblings grew up contemplating questions of race in the most improbable of ways: "Would you marry a white woman?" "What would Neville think if you married a white person?" "Are we a family completely sold on the notion of marriage within the races?" These were all hypothetical questions since the chance of us finding white partners in Jamaica was quite clearly limited by demographics and class.

Not so when I forced these questions on myself in America. The question of what my reaction would be were one of my children to declare love for a white person was not simply a theoretical one any more; it was real.

199

When Sena was five and Kekeli four, attending a preschool in Columbia, they were, quite clearly, minority children. There was one other black child in Sena's class and one black boy in Kekeli's class. The rest of the class was white. The reason for this was that it was a private, white Baptist Church preschool, staffed entirely by white teachers. The fees were predictably affordable as 'private' schools have long been the choice for many white middle to working class families in South Carolina. This pattern can be traced to the years just after desegregation when many whites took flight to enterprising private schools that would remain unblemished by blacks. By the time we got to South Carolina, the last vestiges of such nakedly race-prompted private schools still existed, though overt racial segregation had given way to a new dogma – the evangelical movement's safeguarding of 'traditional' Christian values in the education of children.

Our first concern about sending the children to a largely white school was not the question of whom they would marry, but had to do with our concerns about their racial sense of self. Our conflict was peculiar because unlike most African Americans, we had not grown up in situations where racial segregation was possible. Lorna, growing up in London, could not attend predominantly black schools because they did not exist at the time. She was perpetually a minority among white children and had to negotiate friendships, self-esteem, and the secrets of home in that environment. It is an experience that a number of British-born black women are writing about with sorrow and humour, casting up a fascinating picture of constant and painful self-redefinition.

When I brought home a book by Andrea Levy, an English writer, that traced her life as a "Black" in Britain, Lorna read it with amusement, nostalgia, and some pain. Her years in England were not always easy, but what she understood was that people could live together, albeit with some difficulty, from culturally and racially diverse worlds. For neither of us was the self-sufficiency of living wholly within a minority world ever possible. In Canada, we related to blacks and whites as dear friends because we could not choose to live only among blacks. Such a self-sustaining community of blacks did not exist in New Brunswick. But I also felt that the desire to gravitate towards racially homogenous groupings grew out of a self-limiting defensiveness. Though I understood the need to protect oneself from being consumed by a dominant culture, I could not accept such a route as especially useful or morally comfortable.

Yet in South Carolina, the business of segregation is so thoroughly organized, so unassumingly enacted, that it is difficult not to be sucked into it. No decision made about race is simple. Everything is loaded with questions of self-definition, loyalty, and cultural identity. For us, there were other complications. We were from outside this country and the legacy of racial identity that we carried, while related to that experienced by African-Americans, was also quite different. So we were, quite quickly, faced with a dilemma when it came to schooling the children. We understood the trauma that could come from being a minority in a place where the majority culture is overwhelming. We knew that as the children started to talk about beauty, they would enter into the discourse of the majority. A black child among white children would have no shared language for talking about the beauty of her hair when the majority of the girls would take their cues from the long blonde manes of their Barbie dolls. Our greatest nightmare was having to respond to our children saying that they wished they were white. It is the kind of thing that can happen to children – nothing abjectly traumatic in itself, but so frightening to the parent who is already feeling some guilt for having placed the child in a majority white setting.

Most black children who have lived in societies influenced by western fantasies of beauty and appearance will have, at some point, realized that in some way they have fantasized about being white. For me, the fantasy came when I tried to place myself in the narratives of the books I was reading. I wanted to be one of the Famous Five. In my cowboy adventures, I was not black, I was a white cowboy determined to protect myself from the Red Indians. Whites had all the good adventures. For my sisters, the entry into romance was through Mills and Boon, those British pulp romance novels that they read like they drank water – rapidly, at all times, and with remarkable devotion, as if they could not survive without them. In their bedroom in Jamaica, they had several hundred titles by their mid-teenage years. These formulaic romances had absolutely no black characters. They were all white, all European, and all represented white ideals of beauty. It was no surprise, then, that when we talked about marriage partners, my sisters would declare that they wanted their men to be "tall, dark, and handsome". Apparently, a rather innocuous set of characteristics, but implicit in the clichéd language was the ideal of whiteness. Greek men were the epitome of beauty and my sisters knew this. Here, "dark" did not mean black but dark-haired. My sisters would have known this, too.

I am sure that as they became more and more interested in boys in Jamaica, the ideal had to be compromised, and eventually totally rejected. The rejection would come from the process of imagining the union of this Greek god and themselves. Was that image on the covers of these books? No. The ideal woman, folded into the arms of this flaming-eyed Greek god, was a blond-haired goddess of completely European fantasy. My sisters could not fit into that picture. To participate in the fantasy they had to remove themselves from the picture, and engage in an act of vicarious enjoyment that was particularly remote. They would eventually reject all of this because it ran counter to their reality in Jamaica. There were no Greek gods in Kingston at the time and finding and loving a boyfriend meant choosing from the large pool of black boys, their peers. They had to reformulate their sense of beauty and reject the racial constructions of the books.

In America, my children would not have it so easy. In a majority white culture, where images of beauty as white still pervade the media, and with the ready presence of boys who could pass for Greek gods, their dilemma will be a real one. Were we, as parents, making them negotiate the kind of racial anxieties that had not consumed us when we grew up? So what school for the children?

Our choices were not simple and they stirred up arguments about class, race, and nationalism between Lorna and myself that we probably would not otherwise have had. I could smell my anti-elitist inclinations all around me as we argued. My feeling was: no private education. First, there was the simple fact of the money – we could not afford it; and second, there was the racial implication of the private schools as "white-flight" schools. The assumptions behind the existence of such schools resonate all across America: the assumption that the entry of blacks into the school system means a deterioration of standards in academic work and particularly in discipline. The whole racist business was damaging because the flight of whites from the public schools lead to the sapping of political and community support for those institutions. Whites run the legislature and the education system.

But it is one thing to have a political view of a situation and another to consider the implications for your children. I was resisting the private path because I feared that our children would grow up cut off from the black world. Yet I also had a problem with the assumption that we had a natural affinity with African-American culture. For all that we were all part of the African Diaspora, for all the sense of affinity I felt as a youth growing up in Jamaica, the assumption that I would immediately identify with black culture in America, because I am black, is false. The truth is that my aversion to the powerful influence of American culture, American materialism and American myopia did not recognize racial distinctions. For me, in general, African-Americans had always been Americans first and then Africans. What characterised my African-American heroes – Ali, Angela Davis – was their frontal assault on American pieties.

I know that my children have had to contend with the meaning of racial difference, with negative stereotypes, and with a barrage of good reasons to mistrust white people. It is not that white people are any worse in South Carolina than elsewhere in the world, it is simply that in America there is an inescapable discourse about race that our children have to be equipped to deal with: the racially charged welfare myths, the violence of black society, the myth of the white woman as a cherished sexual prize, the why and why not of a black President, slavery, reparations, the Nation of Islam, affirmative action, race films, the Ku Klux Klan, Barbie dolls, hair, rap music, soul food, high blood pressure, ebonics, and so on and so on. These are minefields for us, never mind the children. Why do we not celebrate Kwanza? Is it worth the hassle to explain that I am Ghanaian and had never heard of Kwanza until I came here? That while I empathize with the intentions, I regard Kwanza as an entirely synthetic American misconstruction of Africa, pretending to an African essentialism that does not exist in reality? How will I reassure my children that saying "We don't celebrate Kwanza, we do celebrate Christmas" to well-meaning, politically-sensitive teachers, when they are wished a "Happy Kwanza" is fine? Do I continue to avoid requests to come and talk about the pillars of Kwanza when my Swahili is weak and I don't really buy any of it? How black is my black? The "race talk" has begun for us.

It began with Barbie. Barbie was major problem for us. Barbie is not just white but is a symbol of crass American commercialism directed specifically at children. Television is riddled with temptations for children, lures into wanting everything they

204

see and forcing parents to define themselves as those who can't afford any of that "foolishness", or those who can (or those who can but won't). The efforts to expand Barbie's racial range, while noble, are undermined by the predominance of the white Barbie in advertisements and on the store shelves. White Barbie is a majority figure and black and brown Barbie must know this when they look at their numbers. Banning television viewing wouldn't work. A visit to any fast food restaurant will confirm how efficient the Disney enterprise is at manipulating children. By giving away dolls and toys that relate to their next "blockbuster cartoon classic", they create the expectation that seeing the latest Disney film is a matter of course rather than a matter of choice, and that possessing the syndicated merchandise is a social norm. When the power of commerce is inflected with questions of race, the "talk" becomes unavoidable.

Barbie and all that Barbie represents became the first instance of my daughters' exposure to American materialism. Barbie must acquire things to be happy. Barbie is fixated on clothes. Barbie is anatomically impossible, but realistic enough to present a model of sexual attractiveness that is Eurocentric, and distorted. Even black Barbie has no backside, no hips. Her mould is exactly the same as that of white Barbie; her nose is the same size – she is just painted brown. The implications for a black child's ideas about beauty are disturbing. And yet I have to wonder whether, as parents, we are making more of this than we should. At one level, saying no to Barbie is about defying the pressure to conform. But is it fair to the child? Are we being alarmist in thinking that having a white doll might seriously damage a black child's sense of self?

In Ghana, my sisters never had black dolls and I don't think any attempt was made to find dolls that looked like them. My parents bought white dolls because dolls were white. We played with these dolls without too much thought about not seeing ourselves in these objects. But the engine of commercialism was not there. There were no television ads showing the dolls as humans, moving around, getting into cars, swimming, in that stiff animation of Barbie advertisements. Were my parents negligent? Were they unaware of the damage that these white dolls and action figures could make to our sense of self? If they were aware, they did not speak about it. I suspect, too, that the difference rested in where we lived. We lived in a world in which our racial identity was taken for granted. So while we saw the images of whites on television, and envied white excitement and materialism, we understood it to be a foreign world, a world defined by nationality rather than race. Ours was not an unambiguous world of racial clarity, but it was clear enough to ensure that our lessons in racial understanding came in spurts – through watching our parents function and then later, through what we read. My father had white friends. So white friends were good. Lesson one. My mother told off a clerk in a London store who seemed quite determined to sell her the cheapest brand of any item she wanted. My mother kept asking for the expensive brands by name, but the exaggeratedly polite white Englishwoman kept saying that my mother would not like that one. Eventually, my mother exploded, told the woman she should not judge people by their race, told her to do her job and show her, the customer, what she wanted. The woman turned red. We smiled sweetly. My mother did not buy the expensive object. Lesson two: stand up for yourself and smell out racial discrimination when it comes in the guise of kindness. There was no long talk.

But we have to talk. At first, my wife and I used codes to distinguish blacks from whites when talking in front of the children. You realize that when you are telling a story about anything that has happened in the South, you have to distinguish the race of the people involved. It affects the meaning of the story: "I met this interesting man today, he really liked my work." "White or black?" We developed euphemisms: "one of ours", "our people"; and then tried longer words: "Caucasians", and so on. Why? Why? Because explicit racial demarcations seemed to us so rude, so impertinent – and ultimately, too adult to impose on our children.

It made us aware of how much we talk about race. In this place, race is so attached to character, to motives, and to interpersonal relationships, that it remains at the core of our discussions. Our lives are complex because we relate to both whites and blacks in social and professional settings and it became almost impossible for Lorna and I to go a day without talking about the racial implications of actions taken, of situations that had arisen. It was hard to keep this from the children, for even the small details of our life were predicated on how we negotiated race in this society.

Our only alternative would be to completely immerse ourselves in black culture and the black world and thereby seek to avoid the problems of race. Some do this, but we would still be aliens in that world, because we are, in America, aliens.

So we are sensitive about race. Yet we did not want this sensitivity to be adopted by our children too early in life, though it was clear that from their earliest years they were encountering race. Sena, when she was four years old, observed that in her class she was different, that she was seen as different because she was one of only two blacks in her class. Within a year, she learned the ritual of racial solidarity, the rituals of difference. At the beginning of the year she did not identify the black boy in her class as a friend or playmate. We observed the way she established friendships with some and denied friendships to others. The reasons were always predicated on personality and behaviour. Near the end of the year, she observed that she and the other black boy were the only blacks in the class. "We are brown," she said. Then she declared him her friend. She gave no reason. We offered a few reasons (other than racial affinity) for her position and she accepted them quietly. It was a sign of growing up, a complicating of her sense of race.

I remember, one day in Jamaica, asking my parents what they would have felt if I had come home with a white woman. My father said it would not be an issue. He would just hope I knew what I was up for. My mother took the question seriously and answered in her brilliantly pragmatic way. Her answer reflected her willingness to recognize that mistakes were part of a successful life. My mother has always believed in trying things, taking a chance in good conscience and being prepared to adapt and adjust if things went wrong. Love, she said, was a funny thing that resisted common sense and logic when it was at its height. Love was so strong sometimes that it could make the impossible work. If love was the driving force, then it could mean that it had overcome the obvious barriers, at least for a time. She would support love, but would also warn that things could change and we would have to change with them.

I am not sure what they would have said had we been living in a country in which, on the one hand, it was demographically possible for such a union to take place but, on the other, had such a profound racial demarcation as America. I am not sure, but I will try my mother's answer if our children ask. I want them to live in a world that allows for people of different races to share spiritually and socially. I want them to feel free to have friends from quite different worlds. I want them to feel confident enough to approach any group and assert themselves. I want them to read Octavio Paz, Maria Rainer Rilke, T.S. Eliot, Kamau Brathwaite, Sylvia Plath, Gwendolyn Brooks, Dennis Brutus, Robert Creely, Homer, and anyone else they can. I want them to feel they can taste any fruit, walk into any place assured of themselves, of their dignity. I am uncertain whether it can happen if they are raised in South Carolina. And this anxiety fills me with guilt. It really does.

But we began very early to talk about the beauty of black

traits, of the colour of the skin, the quality of hair. We try to celebrate these things. Perhaps what we are actually attempting to instill in the children is a comfort with difference, not simply in racial matters but in basic social circumstances. We talk about differences in academic progress, about the individual's capacity to think and make decisions. It is a subtle way of establishing in them a willingness to make their own decisions based on their own judgment.

There may be major battles ahead. Lorna and I have some passionate views that we fear we will impose on resistant children.

Take cheerleading.

The very idea that cheerleading is regarded as an occupation of privilege for girls seems quite absurd to me. The classic model of the successful American high school couple is the male as the star football player and the female as the cheerleader. I have talked to students who have listed "cheerleader" on their resume as a sign of great accomplishment. There seems no general perception that it is a sexist construct because it deprives young women of being a genuine athletes in their own right and institutionalizes a system where women stand on the sidelines and cheer on the real work of the men – not to mention the explicitly sexual framing of their actions. Nobody reports on the abilities and skills of the cheerleader after the game. Yet my daughter had already started to talk about being a cheerleader when she was four.

As with race, the politics of gender in the USA will, we suspect, demand many talks. It is all new territory for us. We attended single-sex schools. The girls played any sport they wanted and found the capacity to be heroes in their own environments. Much of my sporting success was based on the desire to excel among my peers. There was little of the pressure to play sports to prove something to the girls in the school, because there were no girls. The absence of a female presence brought its own strangeness, but there was something in this arrangement that allowed me to develop without constantly contending with the politics of gender.

However, I am not sure I want a single-sex school for my children; generally such arrangements are so alien to America that schools that adopt the system tend to be private and marked by other preoccupations that would probably bother me. But we have talked to Sena about the silliness of cheerleading. It has been my most "bigoted" stance so far, and I realized, even as I declared that she would not be a cheerleader, that in this I was setting her up to be one. I am happy to report that the contagion has passed Sena by. Akua, I am afraid, has not yet fully escaped it.

One thing my parents did well was to understate their opinions. They rarely made rules. We grew up thinking that all our choices were our own and that my parents were not perturbed by our decisions. There was rarely, if ever, any sense that they were scrutinizing our decisions to determine whether they would damage us permanently. Sometimes their attitude seemed like indifference, yet we knew when there was approval, though never did the approval seem like an assertion of their success in guiding us well. Their parenting style was not lax; they just seemed to have the capacity to establish a clear line between that which had to do with children and that which had to do with adults. In their scheme, sexuality, boyfriends and girlfriends, career choices, party-going, athletics, television-watching, and creativity, were our domain. They did not interfere. They set basic limits, which were relaxed more and more as we got older. In retrospect, of course, it is clear that they were deeply concerned about our decisions, but they had a genius for leaving us with the impression that we were in some kind of control.

The issue of television was a perfect example of their style. In Ghana, we had no television. My father would not buy one. He never explained why and we never thought to ask. We just accepted that there would be no television in our house. Though reading was never organized or verbally encouraged, we just started to read a lot and my father and mother fed our hunger for more and more books and would rarely say no to a request for books, comics, and the other useful texts we found in the university bookstore. Television we watched elsewhere. Our neighbours had televisions. So we would ask permission to go next door and watch television. It was all American and British fare, and apart from *The Saint, Bonanza*, and *I Love Lucy*, few other programmes remain in my memory.

In England, we were too poor to afford our own television. So we would continue the ritual: "Can we go upstairs and watch television?" The ritual was always the same. We went *en masse*, not individually. Television was, to us, a communal activity: we saw the same things and talked about them together. When we moved to Bormer Road, we watched *Robin Hood* and *The Saint* in glorious colour on the television in the pub across the street from our house, huddled near the coat racks in the lobby area before the bar proper. When the pub was demolished, it was a great loss – no television, no football, no cricket, no horse-racing. It may have been at that time that I added television to the list of things I would enjoy as an adult. Copious amounts of Kentucky Chicken, chocolate, meat pies, and ice cream were also on that list. All the things that came in rationed supply.

Jamaica changed things somewhat. There, we realized that we could afford a television, but my father did not see it as a priority. We turned to the radio for music, for soap operas like the British radio drama *Thunder in the Straits*, which came on at about ten o'clock in the morning. During the school term, we did not get to hear the unfolding saga, except on days when we were too ill to go to school. Those days were gloriously free: no parents in the house, a brilliant quietness outside and the fascinating rituals of the neighbourhood to observe: the postman chatting up the helpers from gate to gate, the gardener entering the helper's quarters with a calm impunity that was never apparent in the afternoons. Our helper owned the house during the day. I used to enjoy watching her relax in the living room, listen to the radio, use any toilet she felt to use. The class patterns of Jamaican society were most apparent on such days, for a whole other-world of day-workers, gardeners, broom-sellers, water people, electricity people, plumbers, garbage collectors, bottle collectors and scrap collectors would occupy our middle-class neighbourhood. But at ten o'clock, *Thunder in the Straits* would bring everything to a lazy halt – everyone would be listening.

Television was still someone else's world. We would ask to go next door to see a particular show: *Manix, Mission Impossible, Lost In Space, Star Trek, Bonanza*, and so on. But over time we began to see a change in our parents' responses. So we began to ask, "Can we go next door?" There was still a follow-up question – "For what?" but they rarely seemed that interested in our answer. It was a ritual. This was even more evident when the exchange went: "Can we go next door?" "Yes." or "Uh huh" (head still in a book or the newspaper). When the "we" became "I", and the response was the same, we knew that our parents were getting lax in their dotage. It was not long before the new dialogue was even more permissive: "I am going next door." "Uhhuh." This was now just a ritual of politeness – explaining where we would be. By the time I was fourteen, I was simply saying, "I am going out." Occasionally, the follow-up would be "Where?" Details were only important if it was late at night or if there was something about my attire (cricket gear, silk shirt and stinking of Brut, or shirtless) that indicated that they should know. Those were days when the question was asked as a genuine indication of interest. We were now adults.

The television appeared in our home around that time. We had pressed for it, whined for it. A big black and white set. We watched it indiscriminately for a few weeks and then the novelty wore off. The television is not a memorable part of my teenage years because by then I had found so many other things to occupy my time. Television was just a minor diversion.

But this gradual, unexamined movement towards maturity and responsibility was never discussed, never involved any "talk" that I can remember. It was the manner of my parents' parenting. I realize now that they parented without reference to the pontifications of the experts so ubiquitous now on television and radio.

The sex talk is especially new territory for me because I had no such talk with my parents. My mother talked about sex to us, but it was oblique, not as "the talk", but as a matter of course, a passing conversation. I never talked about sex with my father.

And it was not as if I learned about sex late in life. I can't recall a time when I did not know about sex. But what I knew was learned from my siblings and from my friends and cousins. There was no doubt misinformation, but in retrospect there was also some safety in this, in a world without the superabundance of adult-oriented sexual information that presses on the consciousness of contemporary American teenagers.

I have had to admit to myself, though, that were I a thirteen-year-old again, I would regard the sexual world of America today as a heaven on earth. I mean, as a thirteen year old in 1975, living in Jamaica, had I been able to read the statistics of sexual practice among American teenagers in 1997, I would have been so envious. I would. I was completely consumed by sex, with the powerful secret of my desire. I feared death, not because of hell, but because I would not be able to experience sex. I thought that anyone who died a virgin was dying a bitter and cruel death. My longing was intense, consuming and frustrating because I never imagined myself to be attractive enough to convince a girl to give me what I desired.

I have tried to trace my sexual history. The earliest recollections are sketchy, but they have remained with me. They all emerged from the community of children, a world of discovery, but a world that did not involve adults. It would be that way for a long time. I am aware that I am going to have to contend with a quite different reality for my children. I know that I can't turn to my parents' model of sexual understanding, that I must construct one that can cope with the sexually charged world of America today. There is so much more at stake. HIV-AIDS has changed a lot of things. This is a truism, but I don't think my parents would have handled my sexual education the way they did had there been AIDS.

I have to say here that I can only speak of the sexual talk that I got and not what my siblings got. My parents, and here I mean my mother, were always careful about protecting our privacy as children. I know there were secrets about me that she kept from the rest of my siblings. If she did tell them, they were careful not to let me know that they knew. I can also remember, vaguely, my mother pushing my father to talk to my older brother about girl things. I don't know if the talk happened and I don't think I ever will. I know that no such talk came my way. I have no idea, for instance, what my mother told my sister about menstruation, but she must have said something. All I know is that I remained completely baffled by the sanitary napkin ads on television until well into my late teens – those ads with girls running freely through the grass and bottles of blue ink being soaked up by bullet-shaped cotton swabs. I was not given that talk.

But I knew about sex, knew about it for a long time. In Ghana, I remember my brothers and sisters actually holding a conference to determine what to call the penis and vagina. As I have retained or restructured the memory, our aim was to find a secret word that we, as children, could use in front of adults that would leave them in the dark as to what we were talking about. We settled on "nya-nya", which would work for both genders (we were not yet sophisticated about gender politics). The official names for our penises and vaginas, the ones used by our parents, by relatives, and by other adults – the acceptable word in English – was "thing"; as in "Why are you holding your thing?" or "Let me see your thing" or "My thing is hurting me", or "She hit me in my thing". We would have to come to England to discover "willie" and then to the glorious word-crucible of Jamaica to discover a wide and delicious variety of names from the universal cock and pussy, to the very Jamaican buddy and pum-pum. Of course, we never used those names at home. We stayed with "thing", or graduated to the proper anatomical terms. The Jamaican versions were far too graphic, onomatopoeic, and rude. A Jamaican gem, which still appals decent women, is "punani", which sounds like what it is referring to, but a rude version thereof.

What the actual sexual act involved was also quite familiar to me while I was still young in Ghana. There was a cousin of ours who lived in Cape Coast, who was a bit older than the rest of us, and thus had a wealth of knowledge about everything. He knew how to de-shell a snail and carefully shape the shell into a top that you spun with a snap of your thumb and forefinger. It was a messy job, but he made it look like high science. So every time it rained and snails of all sizes came crawling along the long grasses around our house, we would collect them, pluck out the creatures and make these tops. Our cousin knew how to make sophisticated water pistols with the branches of a certain plant that was used for hedges in our yard and in Cape Coast. He would instruct us in the delicate use of a razor blade and needle to construct this brilliant toy. He knew how to use the white sap that bled from the broken stem of the fruit of this tree to make chewing gum. It was a thick, pasty secretion, that when mixed with saliva became quite gummy. The taste was light and not unpleasant. He knew which leaves of which plant were edible. Some were poisonous, as I learned painfully one afternoon.

This cousin knew games with bottle caps; he knew so much. And he knew sex. He knew it with a gleeful exuberance. I don't recall the details, but I do recall his symbol for sex. It went a long way in teaching me something about the physiology of sexual intercourse and the sound of sex. How he knew all this, I don't know, but he showed us how to place a stiff index finger through a circle made with the thumb and forefinger of the other hand and moving the stiff finger in and out. He would then make a sound like "feeba, feeba, feeba". This was sex! We were well-informed.

The complication of my knowledge of sex took place when I was about ten. It precipitated an obsession that would occupy me for the next seven years. It may also have prompted my fascination with literature's ability to speak the unspeakable, to create a world in which taboos were constantly broken and secret things given articulation. It all seems precious now, tied to initiations and first-time encounters. I learned about how other people had sex from books – from one book at first. I have no clear recollection of the plot, but this is no wonder; it was a pornographic book that came into our home through an older teenage friend, Beverly. She was sometimes an all-knowing "cousin", sometimes as protective and fiercely loyal as a sister – an older sister. She did not want me to read this book that she had decided was suitable only for my older siblings. But I pleaded, begged, whined, harassed, harangued, until she relented, swearing me to absolute secrecy. I read and had confirmed all I knew about sex, and more. I remember the constant and uncomfortable erection that crippled me for days. It was terrible because I had not yet learned about masturbation; there was no relief available to me. But I was ten!

It puzzles me that I am startled by the news that many children today know about sex at an early age – as early as ten or eleven. Some suggest earlier. I worry about this. But I can't imagine that my sexual development would have been improved by a talk from my parents at that age. Still, it is hard to know. I had a sense of my parents' moral views and I think that I had some understanding that sex was an adult activity, but it was all implicit. Now I can't see myself avoiding the "sex talk" with my children, and soon.

America does that to you. America is good at letting you know about the demons that lurk behind every act of neglect, every act of omission – of how much you are responsible for every psychological trauma that your children encounter. And these demons multiply themselves with fascinating rapidity. So the talk will come. What is sex, what should be allowed in touching, what a stranger should never do, and so on. We have started already because every teacher, every day-care worker, everyone who the children are left with can be quickly mutated into the camera-startled faces of all those molesters on television – the babysitters, the scoutmasters, the priests, and so on. We accept what may be a myth that society was safer for us in Jamaica years ago. What may be more accurate is that the silence of suffering was more complete. Or perhaps things *were* better. These talks may be more about easing our fears, protecting us from guilt, than about building well-adjusted children. I can't use my parents' model in this country, yet I want to have the kind of relationship that would allow these children to find their own path, make their own secret discoveries. I want to be able to have the relationship that I had with my mother: the kind that allowed me to turn to her in confession and for some kind of assurance and atonement when, at thirteen, I got what I had always wanted. I became a "man".

I cried as I lay in my bed afterwards, my body still slippery with our fluids. She was in another room at the other side of the house. She may have been sleeping, but I was a nervous wreck. The act itself, the build-up to it was exhilarating and my dominant emotion was one of sheer disbelief. I could not believe it was happening. She was about sixteen, a girl who was staying in our home. She discovered my drawings of sexual situations and had teased me about them. I would spy on her showering and then tell her. I did not ask with any hope of her saying yes, but I asked anyway. I asked for sex. She said yes and told me to come to see her when everyone was in bed. I went. I took with me two cups of wine; it seemed appropriate. She drank both cups. The memory is still laced with the muggy scent of wine mingling with the sweat that stuck to the room like a coat of fresh paint. The act was furtive, but that sensation of being completely swallowed up by a swamp of mud is still unforgettable. The acidic taste of wine in her mouth and her calm, coaxing guidance still flit through my mind. I wore a condom and was not helped in wearing it. After ejaculation, I found myself still erect and she pushed me to do it again without the condom.

I left after she turned to sleep. She was light-hearted and quite amused. I don't know if she had found any pleasure in it at all, but she was smiling and even laughing at me. As I stepped to the door, she asked me why I did not stay with her for the night. I panicked at the intimacy, the suggestion of love in this request, and as I explained the danger of this, I sensed her disappointment and it made everything I felt at that moment seem crass and crude. I had already imagined my boast at school. I was not sure to whom I would boast, but it was a trophy. I had felt this in that dark room.

Yet in my bed I was weeping. I realized at that point that I was ashamed. I was ashamed of my betrayal of my mother. I had abused the fact that this girl was sleeping in our home; I had cheapened it all. I was a typical middle-class boy using any means he could find to get sex. I was ashamed of the girl's confession of love, of affection. I was afraid of the strange sense of loss I felt. For me this was the most significant and traumatic moment in my life and I was facing it alone. I'm not sure whether it was this or the guilt that made me go and knock on my parents' door and wake them.

My mother came out. I said I wanted to talk. She led me to the living room. She could tell I was crying. I confessed. I had had sex. I had done it with a girl who was her responsibility. I had done this thing under her roof. I had violated something fundamental. God was furthest from my mind. My fear was what my mother would think, would feel. Yet I felt free to tell her. This said a great deal to me about our relationship, about its closeness. She was calm. She listened, then she said, "It is done. You can't change that. You made a mistake. She did too." I quickly asked her not to punish the girl, not to blame her, that it was my doing, my initiative. She comforted me, told me to learn something from this, something about love and forgiveness. It was her acceptance that moved me, that comforted me. I am sure she told my father about it, but he said nothing to me. Perhaps she told my sisters, but they too said nothing. It remained our secret and I loved her dearly for allowing the secret to stand so solidly between us.

I want to have that kind of presence in my children's lives, but how does one cultivate such a thing? I would never have made this confession to my father but I want my son to be able to confide in me.

The truth, though, is that living in this period in history when information about everything abounds, talking is almost inescapable. We have talked. My son, my daughters, my wife and I have discussed so many things because television and radio raise these issues demanding that we talk about them. I take some comfort in this. But I also know that my children will have their secrets; that they must be allowed to have their individual quests to define who they are in relation to me and Lorna. It will eventually distance them from us; and yet, beautifully, it will allow us to meet completely unique individuals, holding opinions, arguing and being both part of us and separate from us.

CHAPTER 14

making peace

To live in America means to suspend one's shock at certain ways of looking at the world and to start accepting them not as parody ideologies or poorly scripted stand-up jokes, but as positions one must genuinely consider and offer counter-arguments to.

To live in America and to have children in America means to live with the anxiety that your children will come home one day and say that the United Nations is trying to take over America (and the world) and rule it in ways that will lead to the grand Armageddon; that the General Secretary of the UN is the antichrist, seeking to bring about a secularized system of world domination, the legalization of abortion, the destruction of all religions, freedom of worship and the sacred First Amendment, and the abuse of those true American family values that were held so dearly by the pioneering forefathers of this great nation.

To live in American is to live with the worry that your children will come home one day and tell you that the rest of the world is ungrateful and misguided in its mistrust of American values and political might. They may see the rest of the world as defined in development and civilisation by the extent of its contact with America. It might mean living with children utterly convinced of the desirability of unchallenged American power and by its right to impose its new world order of free trade and "liberal" market economics as the one true way, and its right to unfettered consumption and control over the world's resources, especially oil.

To live in America and to have children born there means to live with the fear that they will come home and declare that government funding of education and the arts is creeping communism; that poor people are poor because they want to be poor and that those who are without work just don't want to work, and that it is not a completely bad thing to have the poor with us as it keeps the economy in check. They will tell you that charity, the giving of the rich to the poor – Pampers and baby food, panties and briefs, toothbrushes, sanitary napkins – is the answer to poverty. They will argue that if pride prevents the poor from taking these gifts, then the poor should find their own way out of poverty.

It may be to face children who will come to you and say, "Daddy, why are you still going on about slavery? Slavery was dealt with once and for all during the Civil War. Get over it. Start fighting the United Nations, which is planning to enslave all Americans regardless of their colour." They may tell me that race is not an issue, that they resent blacks who complain about racism, who pretend that white society has not changed totally in its attitudes towards them. They may tell me that blacks who talk so much about Africa should just go back and live there if they like it so much; that they should wise up and realize that the white forefathers of this nation did them a great favour by forcing them out of Africa to become a part of the greatest nation on the earth. My children may tell me that rap music is destroying black society and that affirmative action has caused black suffering in the last thirty years. They may say that it is time for all Americans to return to the world of the 1950s when America was truly a safe and beautiful place and when all the best values of the society were at their most glorious peak.

To live in America and raise children in America means existing with the constant dread that my children will grow up resenting immigrants, particularly those who *won't* speak English, declaring them a burden on society, an unpatriotic and leaching group who just want to exploit "us". They may talk about trying to preserve the American way as if it is a culture that has lasted ten thousand years. And I will have to spend time arguing with these children, trying desperately not to sound like a rabid Marxist when I say things like, "You know, the CIA did systematically destabilize Jamaica and Ghana when I was growing up." They may find my attempts to offer alternative visions as trite, misguided, and irrelevant. It could be hard to argue with my children, hard to offer them anything that will make a dent in their sense of utter self-sufficiency, their sense that living in America is all one must do to experience the fullness of life.

It is not that I cannot accept the likelihood of debates around these issues taking place in my home, but my fear is that the points of disagreement could be so absurdly fundamental, so mutually incomprehensible that I would find it hard to argue, because I would know I was not making any sense. I would be branded a dinosaur without any real evaluation of my beliefs. It certainly does mean living in a world in which only two political views are really available: Democrat or Republican – as if these represent the full range of political options, as if they contain the ultimate synthesis of all the world's polarities.

For most Americans, this litany of anxieties will probably seem a misguided tirade, hardly the reason for great fear. To a majority of Americans, these are simply the facts of living in this society and there is nothing extraordinary about them.

I wrote much of the above six years ago. At the time it seemed like hyperbole, a comic exaggeration of the religiously inflected conservative politics of America. Clinton was still in power; it was before the terrorist attacks now dubbed 9/11; before Bush came to power buoyed by the conservative religious vote; before the war on Iraq; before the whole tenor of politics and culture had changed enough to make my hypothetical portrait of a highly conservative America wholly unironic.

But in these six or seven years other things have changed. My children are now deeply interested in politics. They listen to the radio, read *Time* magazine and the newspapers, watch the news on television. Without prompting they are interested in what is happening in the world. They are full of questions, amused at the way politicians spin issues and sharply attuned to the ironies and absurdities of what they see and hear around them. They are old enough to make me wonder how much their thinking is coloured by my exclamations over some news story. But they are old enough to be clear about who they are.

My son refers to American foreign policy using the first person plural. The first time I heard him do this I wanted to say, 'What do you mean, *we*?' It hit me that whereas I could not easily refer to America in that manner, it was inevitable that he should.

But these conversations made me realise that I, too, am changing. There is a way in which even the most vigilant of minds finds it hard to resist the lure of a Manichean American narrative as central to the meaning of the world. There is no complicated explanation needed for why this should be so.

I feel surrounded by a media that understands the world only through the filter of what is crucial to a particular definition of American interests and embraces the first person plural in overwhelmingly total ways. Ubiquitous and constant in its pressure, it is hard to prevent this norm from taking root. It has brilliant ways of defusing dissent by placing those who hold different views in situations that make these views appear absurd and unworthy of serious consideration. It is what happens to any non-mainstream political idea that gets any kind of airing on the daytime talk shows. If the Ku Klux Klan is regarded as a buffoon-filled organization run by a bunch of unintelligent poor white trash, with the perverse desire to wear funny hats, white sheets, and elaborate insignias, it is because we have seen them reduced to this on television talk shows. Few people take them seriously any more. The result is that the Klan struggles to take itself seriously. Of course, the Klan is still quite alive and capable of creating its own kind of social havoc, but ultimately the image is what counts. It may be good that the Klan has been so weakened by these entertaining talk shows, but they also parody any serious counter-ideas in American politics as a bit of entertainment. It is a process that makes self-censorship an effective social force.

In this world of stark oppositions, my self-portrait as a Third World radical is, of course, itself a parodic distortion. The reality is that I am still struggling to understand my own ideologies in the context of the rather limited spectrum of American discourse. I am an evangelical, bible-believing Christian *and* I like to root for Cuba in its sporting feats. I am an Africanist who believes that the narrative of the Atlantic slave trade is a point of deep connection and source of cultural and ideological affinity for people of African descent all around the world. I am also deeply critical of the essentialism that infects some Afrocentric discourse.

I remain deeply discomfited by America's current imperial pretensions, but I have also learnt that I cannot spend all my time fighting America, because I also have to live in this society. My children may someday look at me in the same way that I regarded my father: a bit of an anachronism trying to survive in a world that was moving away from him. I don't know how it will all work out. Once I would have described myself as a socialist. Now I don't know how I would describe myself, though

I know that here I might as well be from a different planet. Yet I am also grateful for the quality of life I have enjoyed in America while wanting to see my presence here as a contribution to American life.

And we are here now. We are here because there is a job here and now a home, a state of people I care about and feel connected to. Yes, I am at home in South Carolina and comfortable with the idea. So I must face this and try to provide something more complex and enduring for our children. It is hard in this society to be against the removal of welfare and the ending of state-funded education and medical services, and yet to feel that abortion is not the best alternative to an unwanted pregnancy. It is hard to be a Christian who believes in charismatic ideas about that faith but finds the institutions of that faith locked in racism and the crudest forms of material greed. It is hard to be suspicious of some African American schemes for investing financially in Africa and yet be a supporter of affirmative action as a useful and necessary stage in mitigating the consequences of racial discrimination. It is hard to be defined in ways that lie far outside the orthodoxies sanctioned by the society's political rhetoric, but I feel I have to offer a legacy that defies this. It means difference, and perhaps it is their status as the children of immigrant parents that will give them the means to think differently and, perhaps, that is all I desire for my children: a critical mind, a capacity to see beyond this nation's boundaries, and a desire to know more about the world.

ALSO BY KWAME DAWES

Natural Mysticism: Towards a New Reggae Aesthetic
ISBN: 1-900715-22-8, pp. 296; 1999; £14.99

Kwame Dawes speaks for all those for whom reggae is a major part of life. He describes how reggae has been central to his sense of selfhood, his consciousness of place and society in Jamaica, his development as a writer - and why the singer Ken Boothe should be inseparably connected to his discovery of the erotic.

Natural Mysticism is also a work of acute cultural analysis. Dawes argues that in the rise of roots reggae in the 1970s, Jamaica produced a form which was both wholly of the region and universal in its concerns. He contrasts this with the mainstream of Caribbean literature which, whilst anticolonial in sentiment was frequently conservative and colonial in form. Dawes finds in reggae's international appeal more than just an encouraging example. In the work of artists such as Don Drummond, Bob Marley, Winston Rodney and Lee 'Scratch' Perry, he finds a complex aesthetic whose inner structure points in a genuinely contemporary and postcolonial direction. He identifies this aesthetic as being both original and eclectic, as feeling free to borrow, but transforming what it takes in a subversive way. He sees it as embracing both the traditional and the postmodern, the former in the complex subordination of the lyric, melodic and rhythmic elements to the collective whole, and the latter in the dubmaster's deconstructive play with presences and absences. Above all, he shows that it is an aesthetic which unites body, emotions and intellect and brings into a single focus the political, the spiritual and the erotic.

In constructing this reggae aesthetic, Kwame Dawes both creates a rationale for the development of his own writing and brings a new and original critical method to the discussion of the work of other contemporary Caribbean authors.

Natural Mysticism has the rare merit of combining rigorous theoretical argument with a personal narrative which is often wickedly funny. Here is a paradigm shifting work of Caribbean cultural and literary criticism with the added bonus of conveying an infectious enthusiasm for reggae which will drive readers back to their own collections or even to go out and extend them!

Michael Kuelker writes in *The Beat*: 'Dawes is an ideal grammarian for the reggae aesthetic, his voice the estuary where his energies as a poet, professor and one-time musician are poured. He bears a gift, rarer than it should be in academia, for intellectually processing his subject and still yielding enlivening writing...'

Wheel and Come Again: An anthology of reggae poetry
ISBN:1-900715-13-9; pp. Pages: 216; 1998; £8.99

This is an anthology to delight both lovers of reggae and lovers of poetry which sings light as a feather, heavy as lead over the bedrock of drum and bass. If in the past Caribbean poetry seemed split between the English literary tradition and the oral performance of dub poetry, *Wheel and Come Again* brings together work which combines reggae's emotional immediacy, prophetic vision, fire and brimstone protest and sensuous eroticism with all the traditional resources of poetry: verbal inventiveness, richness of metaphor and craft in the handling of patterns of rhythm, sound and poetic structure.

Its range is as wide as reggae itself. There are poems celebrating, and sometimes mourning, the lives and art of such creative geniuses as Don Drummond, Count Ossie, Lee 'Scratch' Perry, Bob Marley, Big Youth, Bunny Wailer, Winston Rodney, Patra and Garnett Silk. There are poems of apocalyptic vision, fantasy, humour and storytelling; poems about history, culture, politics, religion, art, human relationships and love; poems which employ standard Caribbean English, poems written in Jamaican nation language and many poems which move easily between the two. From its birth in the ghettos of Kingston, reggae has become an international musical language, and whilst Jamaicans are inevitably well represented in this anthology, *Wheel and Come Again* reflects reggae's universal appeal with contributors from the USA, Canada, Britain, Guyana and St. Lucia. What all have found in reggae is an art with a rich aesthetic which, like the poetry they aspire to write, speaks to the body, mind and spirit, which compels a state of heightened expectancy with its combination of pattern and surprise: 'Counting out the unspoken pulse/ then wheel and come again'.

Geoffrey Philp writes in *The Caribbean Writer*, '*Wheel and Come Again* is no academic treatise - it is an attempt to hold a dancehall session in poetry, to take readers to the heart of reggae and carry them into the compelling seduction of the drum and bass' (26). This bold assertion, made in the introduction of Dawes's latest work, *Wheel and Come Again*, could have also added the word 'celebration'. And there is a lot to celebrate in this anthology.

NEW FROM KWAME DAWES

Impossible Flying
ISBN: 1-84523-039-6; pp.84; 2007; £8.99

Impossible Flying is Kwame Dawes' most personal and most universal collection, that tells ' family secrets to strangers'. In exploring the triangular relationship between the poet, his father and younger brother, there are moments of transcendence, but often there is 'no epiphany, just the dire cadence of regret' since the failures of the past cannot be undone, and there is no escape from human vulnerability, and the inevitabilities of disappointment, age and death. But from that acceptance comes a chastened consolation.

As ever with Dawes's collections, the rewards come not only from the individual poems, but from their conversations and the meanings that arise from the architecture of the whole. And as for poems themselves, 'they are fine and they always find a way to cope .../ they outlast everything, cynical to the last foot.'

Praise for *Impossible Flying*

Kwame Dawes is one of the most important writers of his generation who has built a mighty and lasting body of work. *Impossible Flying* is surely his finest book of poetry thus far. These poems are both distilled and richly colored. They synthesize rage, grief, pragmatism, and beauty into a love axis so deeply felt and powerfully expressed it startles.

– Elizabeth Alexander
Yale University

In *Impossible Flying*, Kwame Dawes brings Auden's dictum to mind: 'We must love one another or die.' Dawes confronts death, madness, grief and loss with the power of compassion, a fierce determination to honor his family and his beloved Jamaica. The poet's language is vivid and visceral; his courage and honesty blaze a path in poem after poem. This is the music of survival and transcendence. Indeed, the poetry of Kwame Dawes makes the impossible possible.

– Martín Espada

Majestic is the word that comes to mind reading the finely wrought poems of Kwame Dawes' *Impossible Flying*. Indeed, a sublime talent is needed to fashion poems of such capacious grace and energy. They are simultaneously intimate and political, intellectual and blood-filled, elegiac and enraptured: human in the most epic sense. No other poet of Dawes' generation is writing poems this relevant, this revelatory.

– Terrance Hayes

Impossible Flying is Kwame Dawes's most intimate collection to date. The poems are a conversation with his familial past, present and the impending future – of good and sad memories, of births, deaths, and illnesses, of loneliness and intimacies. But above all, it is poetry about relationships of all kinds – not just between family members, but variant selves, identities, and masks. The evocative birth of his son emerges beautifully as a "brown body covered in the soft film of clay", couched ambitions "whispered about being superheroes and flying" flutter in a Hounslow basement, and reflections on "the way fat weighs us and heart swells" are just few examples of Dawes's phrase-making that is always honest, sharp, and deeply resonant.

Impossible Flying flies through territories most poets are not willing to visit – it makes what might be impossible for many, possible for some. Ultimately, the strength of this book lies not only in its exactitude of language and tonality, but also in the way vulnerability is presented in an unapologetic, convincing, and moving manner. The over-coolness of contemporary English poetry can learn a lot from Dawes's lyrical bass-tuned pitch, sermonic narrative style, and intelligent range.

– Sudeep Sen, author of *Postmarked India: New & Selected Poems* (HarperCollins)

All Peepal Tree titles are available from our website: www.peepaltreepress.com; email hannah@peepaltreepress.com Or you can contact us at Peepal Tree Press, 17 Kings Avenue, Leeds LS6 1QS, UK (Tel +44 113 245 1703)